TWAYNE'S WORLD AUTHORS SERIES

A Survey of the World's Literature

Sylvia E. Bowman, Indiana University
GENERAL EDITOR

NEW ZEALAND

Joseph Jones, University of Texas
EDITOR

Jane Mander

(TWAS 178)

TWAYNE'S WORLD AUTHORS SERIES (TWAS)

The purpose of TWAS is to survey the major writers—novelists, dramatists, historians, poets, philosophers, and critics—of the nations of the world. Among the national literatures covered are those of Australia, Canada, China, Eastern Europe, France, Germany, Greece, India, Italy, Japan, Latin America, New Zealand, Poland, Russia, Scandinavia, Spain, and the African nations, as well as Hebrew, Yiddish, and Latin Classical literatures. This survey is complemented by Twayne's United States Authors Series and English Authors Series.

The intent of each volume in these series is to present a critical-analytical study of the works of the writer; to include biographical and historical material that may be necessary for understanding, appreciation, and critical appraisal of the writer; and to present all material in clear, concise English —but not to vitiate the scholarly content of the work by doing so.

Jane Mander

By DOROTHEA TURNER

Twayne Publishers, Inc.   ::   New York

Acknowledgments

Thanks are due to many who have helped me with material and recollections; in particular to Mr. Ian Whitwell of Auckland University for sharing the results of his field work on Jane Mander's northern background; to Mr. Pat Lawlor and Mr. John A. Lee for the use of her letters; to Mrs. Esther Norton Soule and Mr. Monroe Wheeler of New York; to Miss Ada Coates and Mr. Mervyn Sterling of Matakohe and Mr. Edgar Hames of Paparoa who took me through the *Allen Adair* country and to Mr. R. T. V. Linnell for similar help in *The River*'s setting; to Mr. George McDonald, Ararimu's historian, to Miss Brayshay whose legal researches established which house Jane Mander was born in, and to Mr. and Mrs. Allen Reid, present owners of the now verified birthplace; to Jane Mander's cousins, Mr. and Mrs. H. V. Kerr of Whangarei, and to her nieces, Mrs. J. B. Walker and Mrs. R. Campbell; to Mrs. W. Reynolds, Mr. and Mrs. A. H. Pickmere, and Mrs. Florence Keene of Whangarei; to Jane Mander's Auckland friends, Mrs. May Ryan, Mr. and Mrs. Ronald Holloway, Miss Gloria Rawlinson, Mrs. Maud Graham, Mr. Frank Sargeson, and Mrs. T. R. Vernon.

Special thanks are due to Miss Esther Greene, Librarian of Barnard College, and to Mr. Wade A. Doares, Librarian of Columbia University's School of Journalism; to the staffs of the Alexander Turnbull Library and the General Assembly Library and to the latter for its research privilege; to Mrs. W. Lightbody of the Whangarei Public Library and to the staff of the *Northern Advocate*; to librarians at the Auckland Institute and Museum and at the University of Auckland; to Mr. Jonathan Dodd of Dodd, Mead & Co., New York, for research into his firm's dealings with Jane Mander; to the Wellington Public Library for long loans of its stack-room copy of *The Passionate Puritan*; to the Library of Congress, Washington, D.C., for its prompt check of her early writings; to Mr. E. I. McLaren of the Auckland Public Library who made the enlarged print for the dustjacket, and to that library's reference staff for resourceful suggestions and good-humored fetching out of heavy backroom material in a building due for demolition when Jane Mander was using it.

For permission to quote from Jane Mander's writings grateful acknowledgment is made to her literary agents, Christy & Moore of London; to the publishers John Lane, Hutchinson & Co., Robert Hale Ltd., and Whitcombe & Tombs; to the *New Republic*; to New Zealand Newspapers Ltd., for material used from the *Auckland Star*, the Auckland *Sun* and the Christchurch *Sun*; to the Christchurch *Press* for the use of material by Ngaio Marsh and Jane Mander; and to Dame Ngaio for adding her consent. For permission to reprint Katherine Mansfield's review of *The River* acknowledgment is made to the Society of Authors. I have quoted extensively from what Mr. M. H. Holcroft has written of Jane Mander in the *New Zealand Listener*, from Professor Joan Stevens's comments in *The New Zealand Novel: 1860-1965* (A. H. & A. W. Reed), and from Professor Robert Chapman's analysis of the social pattern in *Landfall*, and thank these authors and publishers for their permission. Special thanks are due to Professor Joseph Jones of the University of Texas for very helpful suggestions and editorial supervision during the preparation of this volume.

Preface

When Jane Mander's novels began to appear in the 1920's, New Zealand's response to them affected her writing, more deeply, it could be, than anything that was happening overseas to her or to them. This regrettable story, in various vague forms, has become a legend. Comments of newspapers of the day, and of interested people, are used here in an attempt to determine what did take place between Jane Mander and her own country. To give these details, as I have done in the final chapter, seems a betrayal of the dignity and fortitude with which she bore her side of the affair. But it was after all a duologue, continuously engaging her vital forces; she can be understood only in this context. And what New Zealand said to her is so much in character that through her novels this country is twice revealed: once as she portrayed it and again in its reply to her portrait. These novels of solid realism are the artist's posthumous voice, and each chapter of this study is part of a continuing and changing response to them.

Like her contemporaries, Katherine Mansfield and the painter Frances Hodgkins, she was an expatriate during her creative years. I have touched only briefly on the implications of this; studies of several of our expatriates have by now revealed most of the griefs and hazards of the condition these three pioneered. In particular, Dr. E. H. McCormick's *The Expatriate: A Study of Frances Hodgkins and New Zealand* contains much that is analogous to Jane Mander's case. Frances Hodgkins was, as the author points out, "a more conventional woman and a more representative figure than Katherine Mansfield." So, too, was Jane Mander. They were alike also in trying to remain part of their uncomprehending country. Jane Mander returned to it in middle age, her talent deflected and shriveled, to battle as best she could for artists here. Frances Hodgkins, the only one of the first three to save both life and talent, finally accepted the severance New Zealand forced on her. Then, as an elderly, distinguished European painter in the 1930's she spoke as a European to a young New Zealand painter: "They're lovely people, the New Zealanders, so hospitable and so charming. But for God's sake don't talk to them about art!"

This dissociation by pronoun was prevalent for some decades;

as the temper of the country became known, young New Zealand artists practiced it in advance of repudiation—when they dropped in at our firesides, or we at theirs overseas, and hard things had to be said about this country, they called us "you," though they did not identify themselves with any other adopted country. The use of the pronoun was almost a cultural shibboleth. This is now changed, and Jane Mander's criticisms of her country, spoken always from within the family, have a modern ring. She was, in any case, "quite without hauteur" as one Auckland interviewer noted with astonished relief in 1932, the year she came home; and like a true daughter of the democratic, unprivileged north, she assumed no patronizing airs. More fundamentally, though, as I think all her writings show, she believed too much in New Zealand's social experiment, had too actively promoted it, to dissociate herself. She knew no reason why effective concern for the underdog and the removal of entrenched privilege should not coexist with the human diversity and appreciation of *métier* the arts need. Historically she has yet to be proved right: the arts have been fostered in unequal societies and have petered out in crusades for human justice; cultures seem to have leaned one way or the other, as if humanity's two main needs were incompatible. I believe, though, that most New Zealanders want a solution only on Jane Mander's terms, holding the local element she assailed to be an unfortunate extra the immigrants brought in, not organic to the experiment. The redemption of Alice Roland—the theme as I see it of her first novel—surely presaged that the real barrier to the arts in New Zealand would be those same obdurate self-limitations in the national character that might have derived from Alice. We have had writers more persuasive, but scarcely any so pertinent.

I have extended the biographical survey—the first chapter— beyond the usual limits of the Twayne series because the only other published account of Jane Mander is the 1,000-word entry in *An Encyclopaedia of New Zealand* (1966). The facts have been gathered slowly from scattered and fragmentary sources. I cannot complain: I could have had them from Jane Mander if I had followed up my Auckland encounters with her, if I had not been obsessed, like most of my generation, with the ideal of Europe as our only immediate answer. The few who did preserve local and family records in the face of massive indifference have earned our gratitude, and I have given full notes as to known sources and gaps to help the now active research to make up for lost time.

The Story of a New Zealand River has the second chapter to itself, though certain aspects of it are held over for discussion within the framework of the later novels. The three other New Zealand-based novels are studied in the third chapter, each separately in the first instance, and then in phases to which more than one of them contribute. The two novels with an overseas setting which occupy the fourth chapter indicate what issues the author took with her when forced from the local scene; they complete the portrait of the fictional self and help define her feminism—if that is what it was. All these novels have been unobtainable for many years, except *The River*, last issued in 1960. (I have chosen this abbreviation of the cumbrous title from three the author herself used.) The University of Auckland is preparing the first reissue of *Allen Adair*, and the two others based on New Zealand will be restored in time. Meanwhile, so far as I know, it is only in the Alexander Turnbull Library that a student can read all six. I have therefore quoted enough dialogue, description, and narrative for readers to form conclusions and have left it to a later chapter to set out the various influences that shaped the novelist: the social, religious, and literary background of childhood; the possible effects of time spent in Australia and the United States; and the difficulties of formulating a style. This fifth chapter is a necessary compilation of topics and opinions, interrelated mainly by the light they throw on the novels. Time sequence takes over again in the final chapter in the account of New Zealand's critical estimates of Jane Mander from 1920 on.

No unpublished manuscripts are held by her executors or literary agents. Her letters, articles and reviews are important now mainly as sidelights on the novelist's mind—facility never came to her, nor the grace of style that makes small pieces glow. Her reputation will continue to rest on the six novels that came out of a short productive period. Because I cannot see that her shorter writings will be collected for publication, I have included in the notes three pieces of special significance: the whole of "A Diary of Evolution" and most of "Sheltered Daughters," both from the *New Republic* of 1916, and a very short unpublished reminiscence.

To Jane Mander's younger sisters, Mrs. A. V. Cross of Whangarei and Mrs. A. G. Gummer of Auckland, both of whom died in 1970, I have owed much more than a biographer's usual thanks, for their patient help in reconstructing a singularly undocumented story.

As literary executor, Mrs. Cross gave full permission to quote from the writings, lent me the only extant family letters—those written her from New York—and the author's file of published articles and reviews of her books. These papers Mrs. Cross then handed to the Auckland Public Library to join the scripts of the last four novels, which Jane Mander placed there; the letters remain in the care of Mrs. Cross's daughter, Mrs. J. B. Walker of Kerikeri.

The Manders learned to live without written record, for reasons self-evident in their story; but there is perversity in the way fire, negligence, and even official destruction have removed Jane Mander's traces from schools and newspapers she was associated with, as surely as green pasture has obliterated her gumfields and bush; and the New York studio which took the dustjacket photo reports that the plate was one of a batch called in by the United States government during World War I for making explosives. She did her share of destruction among personal records, the habit of traveling light being joined to a strong respect for other people's privacy. When she says (in her "Preface to Reminiscences"), "I don't claim to have been told more secrets than any other woman, but I do claim to have kept more secrets than most women," she means it very seriously. She loved to know—her questions often took her friends aback—but she did not see their personal lives as hers to use, except maybe as transfigured in a novel. Her typewriter was shackled the moment it mentioned a real name, as is apparent in her radio scripts about overseas people: she had talked with most of the novelists of her day, from Frances Hodgson Burnett to James Joyce, and had known a number of conspicuous people very well indeed, but her comments are about as colorful as an entry in *Who's Who*. On the same principles of privacy all her friends' correspondence and the main interfamily letters were destroyed.

The late Mr. O. A. Gillespie of Wellington, who wrote the entry on Jane Mander in *An Encyclopaedia of New Zealand*, also made radio plays of *The River* and *Allen Adair* and compiled the Radio Portrait broadcast in 1955. He contemplated a biography, but other writing occupied him till his death, and any material he assembled has not been forthcoming. For the Radio Portrait he had Mrs. Cross's letters, besides two or three of uncertain ownership, some that presumably arose out of his acquaintance with Jane Mander and others he solicited from her overseas friends. I have relied entirely on the accuracy of quotations from letters in his script, though

Jane Mander's lifelong reluctance to date correspondence makes them more hazardous in use than he always realized. Both Mr. Gillespie's accounts of Jane Mander are lively and, to my mind, essentially true. His only serious misconception is one shared by her relatives and friends—that the novel written in Whangarei was revised until it became *The River*. She was always laconic about work in progress, but in certain interviews among her clippings are remarks indicating an entirely fresh start made some time after settling in New York. I could never convince myself that this point had been made or transcribed attentively enough to warrant an upset of established belief; but in 1968 Mrs. Margaret Scott, manuscripts curator in the Alexander Turnbull Library, searching unsorted papers of the late Mr. Johannes Andersen, found biographical notes Jane Mander had written in 1935 for the *Author's Week Booklet* (which did not use them), and here she makes the point with emphasis. This is confirmed in a similar note written in 1938 for the late Mrs. Ethel Wilson of Auckland, acquired later in 1968 by the chief librarian of the Turnbull. All Jane Mander's scattered utterances fall into place around these two hard-core statements on *The River*'s origin, dispelling our long-standing impression that she was occupied in New York between 1912 and 1917 in removing outspokenness from a novel already written in New Zealand. (John Lane did ask her in 1917 to drop two passages from *The River*; apart from that it was published as first submitted.) The significance of this is that if *The River* was conceived and written in New York, we must look more closely at her years in that city, and this I have tried to do.

DOROTHEA TURNER

Karekare, Auckland

Contents

Chronology

1877 Mary Jane Mander, eldest of five children of Francis and Janet Mander, is born at Ramarama near Drury, Auckland, on April 9.

1881 Moves to Awhitu, southern entrance to Manukau Harbor, where father begins bush-felling.

1883 Enters primary school at Wellsford, north of Auckland.

1885 Leaves for Port Albert in April, but is soon at Pukekaroro near Kaiwaka, the setting of *The Story of a New Zealand River*; returns to Port Albert probably during 1888.

1889 Enrolled at Onehunga primary school in March; lives at Mangere.

1892 Returns to Port Albert; no high school available; begins teaching in Port Albert primary school.

1896- Lives at Avondale in outer Auckland while father mills in the
1900 Waitakeres; teaches at Devonport, Otahuhu, and Newton West primary schools; continues night study for matriculation and passes in 1897.

1900 Moves to Whangarei, resigns from teaching; father and brother mill at Puhipuhi.

1902 Frank Mander promotes a Whangarei paper, closes it down to buy the main paper, the *Northern Advocate*, where Jane is strenuously occupied for four years; he defeats the sitting member for Marsden, is in Parliament for twenty years in Massey's Reform party.

1906 Frank Mander sells the *Northern Advocate*; he builds the Hatea Street house where Jane begins a novel.

1907- She visits Sydney in 1907, and again around 1910 for more
1911 than a year; between visits works on *North Auckland Times* in Dargaville; in Sydney is occupied with freelance journalism, music, and languages, is befriended by the W. A. Holmans and encouraged to go to overseas university. Returns to ask parents' support for study at Columbia University School of Journalism.

1912 Leaves New Zealand in June for New York with stopover in London where novel is rejected by four publishers; enters

School of Journalism at Columbia University in September as first-day pupil; lives at Whittier Hall; completes first two years with distinction.

1913   Spends summer at Lake George, New York, with friends re-writing novel which is again rejected, then scrapped.

1914   Chaperones student friends, Esther and Rose Norton, to France for the summer; drafts *The River*.

1915- Withdraws from full degree course; continues writing. Joins
1916   suffrage campaign for New York State referendum; begins attending Washington Square Players and Provincetown Players; finds paid employment with a preparedness day committee, then with National Guard Relief.

1917   Apartment in Waverly Place off Washington Square, administrative post with Red Cross; *The River* submitted to John Lane.

1918   *The River* accepted by John Lane.

1920   *The River* published in New York and in London six months later; leaves Red Cross.

1921   *The Passionate Puritan* published in New York.

1922   *The Passionate Puritan* published in London and *The Strange Attraction* in New York.

1923   Moves to London; *The Strange Attraction* published there.

1924- Novels poorly received in New Zealand; *Allen Adair* (1925)
1932   is the last with New Zealand setting; *The Besieging City* (1926) has a New York setting and *Pins and Pinnacles* (1928) a London one. Reads for publishers; then adviser and English editor for Harrison of Paris, seeing their volumes through the press. Completes one more novel but apparently destroys it after rejection.

1932   Returns to Auckland in October; her mother dies shortly before her arrival. She has contract for another novel and reminiscences, but care for her father, who dies in 1942, and her own poor health prevent substantial writing or return overseas. Actively befriends younger New Zealand writers. *The River* republished in 1938 to meet new local demand.

1947   Now an invalid; moves to Whangarei to be near brother and sister.

1949   Dies at Whangarei on December 20.

1960   *The River* reissued with help from the State Literary Fund.

CHAPTER 1

A Life in Three Worlds

To Jane Mander fiction was the natural medium for giving and receiving truth about the human race, in which spirit she read widely throughout her life, enjoying diversities of style and background in novels as she relished them in people; but *The Story of an African Farm*, built from the unpretentious materials of an outlandish environment, was her omen. There is no record of when she first came upon this book—probably later than the women in *The Story of a New Zealand River* who read Olive Schreiner in the wilds of the Kaipara in the 1880's—but she is known to have urged it constantly on her friends at Columbia University in the years when she was drafting her own script, and to have seen it as up to her to try to provide similarly for her own new country.[1]

As a Mander she was habituated to untried situations and virgin territory; a bold attack on these was a matter of necessity rather than of presumption. Her father's way of making a home for his bride had been to buy a piece of land with some of the world's largest timber trees growing on it and to set to work with a few simple tools and square, hand-forged nails. This house, which was Jane Mander's birthplace, is still comfortably occupied.[2] When he turned from settler to lumberman he moved many times, providing his children with the privilege of learning how man assembles a home from the materials around him. Through subsequent phases of his life also Frank Mander was the embodiment of the truth of André Siegfried's observation that "The colonials, moreover, are generally men of mingled strength and simplicity. Their strength makes them unconscious of obstacles, and they attack the most delicate questions much as one opens a path through a virgin forest with an axe." [3] Heredity, example, and necessity built the daughter's practical courage which she exercised in a number of ways before bearing it into writing.

By birth Jane Mander was more native than most Pakehas (non-Maoris) of her generation—hence, perhaps, her assurance in interpreting her country. Both sets of grandparents reached New Zealand ahead of the main tide of immigration, and they arrived in circumstances that committed them totally. Her father's parents, John Mander and his wife Mary (née Amphlett) came from Worcester in the *Ramillies* in 1847 in a contingent of Fencibles—British servicemen accepting their discharge in the colony where their presence as settlers at strategic points would give security against possible attack by the Maoris. The Manders were detailed to Onehunga on Manukau Harbor, six miles across the isthmus from Auckland Harbor; here Frank Mander, their fifth child, was born the next year, 1848.[4] The family did not prosper, the terms being tough for a man who had used up his best strength in the services. Frank supported himself from the age of ten, after less than two years' schooling, by farm labor and prospecting, until by the 1870's he was able to take on property near his parents, now near Ararimu, thirty miles south of Auckland. The district's land titles show him moving mysteriously around, changing holdings, as if even then he was more interested in felling trees than in the farming his neighbors aimed at.[5]

The maternal grandparents migrated from Yorkshire in the *Shalimar* in 1859; William Kerr was of a Scots family, not long settled in England, but his wife, a Morley, was wholly English. They brought with them a strong belief in literacy and a practiced ability to maintain it whatever their livelihood. After shrewdly biding his time in Auckland for two years, William Kerr took his young family to a holding at Ramarama, at the corner of the Great South Road and the Ararimu turnoff—promising land and on the only metaled road in the province, the military highway through to the Waikato River.

They had been there only two years when the raids of the later Maori Wars came right into the area, and they were hurried to Drury for protection after burying a few household goods in the orchard; the Maoris ransacked the dwelling before the farm became a point of defense. Lasting peace soon followed. The Kerrs dug up their humble treasures, and Jane Mander has recounted how her mother's share of these trekked with them through her own childhood.[6] Janet Kerr was twenty when she and Frank Mander were married by a Congregational minister in her parents' house, in May, 1876. Frank Mander now had a hundred acres nearby on the Great South Road, where he had been building his house with massive totara planks. Mary Jane Mander was born here on April 9, 1877, and was cared for by her mother's dear friend and capable midwife, grandmother Mary Mander.

The year 1877 is better known for the great Education Act, which removed the provincial system's anomalies and established New Zealand's system of national education which was open to all— "free, secular and compulsory." And in 1877 Kate Milligan Edger completed her Bachelor of Arts degree at Auckland University College, receiving almost as a matter of course a diploma which reputedly made her the first woman B.A. in the British Empire. Her father was the Reverend Samuel Edger of the Albertland Special Settlement Scheme already occupying the Kaipara areas where Jane Mander was to spend most of her girlhood. Dr. Edger had persuaded the Auckland Grammar School to let his daughter read with the sixth-form boys; the school soon extended the privilege and delivered to the university a number of girls as sternly grounded as their brothers. Scholarships provided a clear run for exceptional ability; all a girl of Jane Mander's generation needed beyond this was a father with enough belief in education to allow her access to it. Teachers and ministers were conspicuous among those first fathers; "society"—or Remuera, to use Jane Mander's synonym— stood aside for a long time, committing its daughters to nonacademic private schools; and there were the struggling poor who needed their girls' labor in cash or kind as soon as compulsory education would let them go. But Jane Mander was born into that middle class for whom certain possibilities existed—a notion her family never lost its grip of, though poor as the poorest at times. Her young uncle, Walter Kerr, pulled himself out of Ramarama by night study and farm work first to the university in Auckland, then somehow to Cambridge, returning, with a creditable degree, to become a schoolteacher in New Zealand with writing as a sideline.

The educational auspices around the birth of the academically gifted Jane Mander were no match for her father's unsettled enterprises and his settled ideas about women; she snatched a total of four or five years' schooling here and there. Yet the worst one can ultimately say of Frank Mander's career, as it affected his eldest child, is that it probably deprived New Zealand of a remarkable headmistress of a girls' secondary school. The next two children, Frank Herbert (1878) and Carrie (1880) were born in Ararimu, farther up the valley, and in 1881 they all left the district, which ended Janet Kerr's hopes of a settled home with Frank Mander. He had sold out to buy a sawmill and a small piece of bush at Awhitu, near the southern entrance to Manukau Harbor. Jane, nearly five, was torn from a life in a fixed rural community among all her grandparents and their friends to become a campfollower of bush-felling.

She estimated that they moved twenty-nine times while she was growing up; relatives have put it higher, but nobody kept a tally. The moves were often sudden, usually desperately uncomfortable, and invariably determined solely by the needs of her father's business. Sometimes they could not live with him on the site, minimal though their requirements were, and during part of the Awhitu time they were deposited in a cottage in Onehunga. He came in there one Sunday evening, after the children were in bed and Monday's wash put to soak, to tell his wife that they were moving up into the north in the morning.

His first Kaipara bush was near Wellsford where the elder children went to school for over a year, leaving for Port Albert in 1885, and moving on shortly to Pukekaroro, near Kaiwaka on the Otamatea River. An old boyhood friend, Samuel Bradley of Onehunga, began to back Frank Mander without joining or in any way supervising him in the bush, and before the turn of the century Mander and Bradley were a prominent firm with offices in the center of Auckland. Scorning written agreements and holding nothing so sacred as the spoken word, the two men maintained a twenty-year partnership with nothing on paper between them.[7] The insecurities of Jane Mander's childhood were only material ones; in her father as in her mother she met with an incorruptible code, and similar standards prevailed among settlers in these northern communities. It was true, as she often said proudly afterwards, that she had met all types in the camps and mills; but in the closer circles she had never to reckon with deceit or betrayal, nor had she run into circumstances that would persuade her to use them. One of her later friends said "If I had to sum Jane up in one word, I would say she was honourable."

An old photo shows the treeless point on the Otamatea River where the Manders lived,[8] their own small house a few feet above three smaller ones on the beach by the logging tramline (whose piles are still standing—all other traces have gone). The bush was back in the heights around the Pukekaroro Mountain. Access to the point was mainly by water, and though Jane did sometimes walk the rough miles through to the Kaiwaka school, her mother taught her most of the time.[9] After about two years they headed back to Auck-

land, living at Port Albert on the way and with the Kerrs at Ramarama, the eldest daughter, now about eleven, carrying in her mind
the background of *The River*.

By 1889 she was at the Onehunga Primary School, a long way
from the house their father built them in Mangere, but a fine school
in a settled area. While her father took it easy for a change and even
talked of retiring, she reached Standard VI, the end of compulsory
schooling and the point of decision about higher education. At this
moment Mander and Bradley "in consequence of some misunder-
standing with the Kauri Timber Company as to some other bush
areas . . . were compelled to enter business again, and built a mill
at Port Albert."[10] The family returned to the Kaipara to live on the
beach in a corrugated iron shed which had once been a general
store. There was no high school in this district; Jane, at fifteen,
went instead as probationary teacher into the local primary school
whose remarkable headmaster, George Reid, so encouraged her
solitary studies that four years later, after a term or two at night
school in Auckland, she was able to pass matriculation, an exam
usually taken only after three full years at high school. For all its
hardships, Port Albert, as the focal point of that struggling band of
idealists, the Albertlanders, gave the Manders a period of consoli-
dation within a singularly interesting community.[11]

Leaving their mill working there, Mander and Bradley moved in
1896 to Nihotupu in the Waitakere Ranges, only fourteen miles
from Auckland, where a few massive kauri trees remained on slopes
hitherto deemed too steep; they put in a tramline which lowered the
timber nine hundred feet in a mile, considered a record. The family
lived at Avondale, halfway between the bush and the city; Jane
taught in Auckland primary schools, often staying with her grand-
father Kerr who now lived in the city; she passed her teachers' exams
well, but university, it was held, could not be afforded. When the
Nihotupu kauris were finished, the firm moved on with the mill to
attack the remains of the great Puhipuhi forest thirty miles north of
Whangarei. The family home no longer needed to be near the bush,
since Frank Mander was delegating management to his son; they
settled therefore in Whangarei, the largest town in the north, with
seven thousand people—a long overnight boat trip from Auckland,
but a complete place, peaceful and pretty. Here they moved
through several houses on a comfortable level as Frank Mander prepared to adopt Whangarei, or to ask it to adopt him. He had re-

cently written of himself: "Mr. Mander has not taken any active part in political or municipal affairs, although he is an enthusiastic member of the National Association, as his time has been fully occupied in fighting the battles of life; the only hobby he indulges in is the pursuit of art, and although he is not an artist by education, he has to some extent developed his artistic endowments."[12]

In the general election of 1902 he contested the Marsden seat for Massey's Opposition and defeated the sitting member by fifty-eight votes. His daughters had thought him a "silly old ass" for putting himself forward in a district when he was a newcomer; they had not allowed for the way his good repute—and indeed the whole family's—had carried throughout the north. The country's political mood, moreover, was beginning to turn against the Liberal government's long reign; but above all, perhaps, the Marsden electors required a candidate who would fight for the neglected north with the conviction and aggression needed to make an impact on Wellington. They were not convinced the sitting member had done his utmost, but Frank Mander would. As indeed he did. From his maiden speech where he described simply the plight of settlers denied the railway coverage given the South Island,[13] he went on for twenty years to fight for the area he knew, a respected but by no means notable member of a series of undistinguished Parliaments, and on retirement he was appointed to the Legislative Assembly.

In 1902 he acquired the *Northern Advocate*, the north's major newspaper. His proprietorship gave his daughter the only qualification by which a woman could then enter journalism, though he may not have envisaged her moving in as she did. Officially she was a subeditor and reporter; when needed she could write "Advice to Mothers" or help with the machinery. "At times I ran the department singlehanded from leaders to proofs, and the proudest boast of my life is that I once brought out the paper four days running without a mistake and caught the four o'clock train."[14] In 1906 Frank Mander built an appropriate house, set in several acres a mile from the town's center.[15] Flat fields provided for a fine garden and the inevitable horses, and behind them, down a steep slope, was sheltered mooring on a tidal river. The house was topped by a round tower which Jane Mander appropriated. There she began a novel, relieved to be away from the paper, which her father sold this same year.

He built of the best kauri, furnished the drawingroom in a pink and green scheme of lasting materials, chose the statues for the front garden, and put a banquet table in the long diningroom. Here was his chance to atone to his womenfolk for their years of discomfort and insecurity—if only he could have brought himself to consult them. The house was soon notorious for the dark inconvenience of its kitchen area: outside help hired on formal occasions only added to the congestion, and the daughters remembered with hilarity the dinner given for Sir Joseph Ward, then prime minister, when the order "Clear soup for Sir Joseph" rang down the line of waiters to end in chaos around the little cooking stove. Laughter did often prevail, for the sisters knew how to be happy together, and during their father's long absences in Wellington life was relaxed; but there was no dodging the realization that prosperity had not solved everything. Jane Mander firmed up her determination to go; her mother moved toward the chronic invalidism of defeat.

Jane went to Sydney first, only twelve hundred miles away, but in size and sophistication another world to a New Zealander. There she met writers and artists, took music lessons, and freelanced a little. She went home for Christmas in 1907. Wanting occupation and money for another trip she began to edit Dargaville's *North Auckland Times* which competed with the *Wairoa Bell* run by John Stallworthy, member of Parliament for Kaipara, for the few hundred possible subscribers around the Wairoa River. *The Strange Attraction* harks back to journalism in Dargaville, but a factual record of her stay is elusive;[16] the paper's files were lost: some say that fire got them, others that they were thrown into the river. Jane Mander was over thirty now, still far from her overseas goals and distant even from what centers of stimulus existed in her own country; she wrote despairingly to the *Triad*,[17] the critical bohemian monthly in the south which was the lifeline for her kind, but by the end of 1909 she was back in Sydney. This time she became a friend of the W. A. Holmans—he was on his way to becoming premier of the New South Wales Labour government, and his wife had been a small-town do-it-all-yourself journalist like Jane. Now she was mixing in circles where viewpoints and speculations might be tossed around without personal hurt to loved ones and consequent self-reproach; it was just what she needed, and it was years overdue. At this point she had an affair with socialism, sending articles back to Wellington's *Maoriland Worker*, but signing them "Manda Lloyd," presumably to spare her father. The Holmans encouraged her to go

farther overseas; American friends in Sydney convinced her that
theirs was the land of opportunity for women and that Columbia
University's School of Journalism was the place to begin. She came
home to persuade her parents, needing their financial help to supplement her savings, and wanting their blessing with it, if possible.

Her parents, being quite within the norm, would rather have
sheltered than subsidized her; many a man of that era is remembered replying, "Thank you, I am quite able to provide for my
daughter," to the suggestion that his bright girl was worth educating. Jane finally won her point, however, at least as to finances—
their blessing was dubious. Frank Mander decided to pull out of
Whangarei, though continuing to represent it, and in March, 1912
went with his invalid wife and two daughters to live in Auckland—
the youngest daughter was married in Whangarei. Jane stayed behind to clean up six years' accumulation, the most they had ever
had, and the bonfires burned. In June she headed for New York
allowing for a stopover in London. "I took with me a first novel, not
the Story of a New Zealand River, as has been erroneously stated.
This book was turned down with admirable promptitude by four
publishers. Among them was the late Mr. Heinemann, who saw me
personally, and gave me half an hour of the best criticism and advice
I have ever had from anybody. It was a sad pity that I did not afterwards send the New Zealand River to him."[18]

But what were four rejections at a moment like this? "In the year
that I first went to London, straight from the barren wastes of Victorian Philistinism, the year 1912, the Russian Ballet was there with
Nijinsky and Karsarvina, with *Spectre de la Rose, Narcisse, Petrous-
chka, Les Sylphides, L'Après-midi d'un Faune, Scheherazade, Le
Sacré du Printemps* and the rest of the wonderful repertoire . . .
and if I could choose to live again three weeks out of my past I
should chose those three weeks in London with their revelation of
beauty such as comes to one only once in a lifetime."[19] By September she was in Whittier Hall, enrolled as a first-day student in Columbia University's School of Journalism.

I   *New York*

So many years of negotiation and publicity had preceded the
school's opening that a good deal was known of its intentions, even
in New Zealand. Joseph Pulitzer had lodged some of the money for
it as far back as 1903, but long absences from America and failing

health delayed his agreement with the university as to its organization, and by the time it opened it was not the first in the country as had been envisaged. The president of the University, Dr. Nicholas Murray Butler, had been anxious that a professional school, especially of such a new kind as journalism, should conform to the usual academic pattern; Pulitzer was determined that it should keep one foot in the highway of events, which had been a reason for his choosing Columbia, whose reputation had never been that of an ivory tower. His physician and amanuensis, Dr. George W. Hosmer, wrote to Dr. Butler that there must be admittance for students without previous collegiate credits. "Upon any other basis, there would have been excluded from such a school nearly every distinguished journalist I ever knew. Mr. Pulitzer could not have been admitted, nor could Mr. James Gordon Bennett, neither the first nor the second, nor Horace Greeley, nor the earliest and most famous of our newspaper men, Ben Franklin himself."[20] Fortunately for Jane Mander it went the Pulitzer way. The word "None" in her big, clear writing answered the entry form's question: "What high school or institution of equivalent grade have you attended?"[21] She mentioned briefly her past teaching and subediting, and across the bottom of the form went the acceptance: "Recommended for admission as non-matriculant, subject to Dean Gildersleeve's approval. J. W. Cunliffe."[22]

While she was packing in Whangarei the university authorities were still arguing about whether women should be allowed in at all; only long diplomacy had won them what limited entry they had to Columbia. Dean Virginia Gildersleeve, principal of Barnard College, recalled that the English Department's Professor Brander Matthews "was very obdurate for a long time. In recompense for having contributed two great scholars to the Faculty of Political Science, Professor James Harvey Robinson in History and Professor John Bates Clark in Economics, Barnard College had secured the admission of women to graduate courses under that Faculty. There remained a number of other departments in which the doors were closed."[23] The School of Journalism was in fact the first of the professional schools to admit women; by a last-minute compromise, Barnard College was to undertake the two years of collegiate preparation for women, who would then join the men for professional subjects. The elements of chance that had abridged Jane Mander's New Zealand education were switching themselves to her side at this stage. Even her nationality may have helped bolster her application; in 1934 when she was home again and arraigning her compatriots for backsliding, she wrote:

Twenty years ago when I first went to New York to Columbia University I was astonished to find myself regarded as an "event of importance," the first New Zealander to enter there as a student. I was an "object of inspiration," and was subjected to exhaustive questioning because of the excitement over what my country "stood for." We were then leaders of social legislation! We were high-minded about the value of human life! We were socialism without bloodshed! We were Utopia materialised! Yes, all that. A positively exciting country! And its glory reflected itself on me, and I became a university pet, and even the entrance rules were amended to meet my "case," such was the enthusiasm.[24]

Her professors of history were James Harvey Robinson and David S. Muzzey. The former had been looking with discontent on current methods of teaching history and was writing books which were to revolutionize it. Charles Austin Beard, her lecturer in politics, became the center of controversy in 1914 with his eighth book, *An Economic Interpretation of the Constitution of the United States;* in 1917 he resigned from Columbia in protest against the dismissal of two colleagues (with whose views he disagreed) and forthwith organized the New School for Social Research in New York with John Dewey, Thorstein Veblen, and James H. Robinson. A humanitarian radical, as Jane Mander was, could not have been better suited; it was a singular piece of luck that the aspect of the university so congenial to her—and the one she mainly availed herself of— was bound up with the functional-sounding course in journalism which had made her a case for leaving home. Her subjects were English, French, history, introductory science, philosophy, and politics; except for a B in history in the first half-year, she had grades of A right through, topping her class.

The registrar of Barnard at the time, Miss Anna E. H. Meyer, wrote recently that she remembered Jane Mander "very well, partly because she was our first student from New Zealand, and partly because of the impression her personality made on me. She was much older than most of the students and she knew very definitely what she wanted to accomplish." Miss Meyer stated also that the prejournalism course at Barnard was a "very stiff one," consid-

erably more exacting than the regular bachelor of arts course.
"There would have been little time for her to put into extra-curricu-
lar activities, many of which might have seemed infantile to her."[25]
Jane Mander's only comment on the study hours is in a report home
of triumphant exam results, concluding, "but Oh Lord, the grind
is pretty bad." Nevertheless she was writing: in the summer of 1913
the family of Katherine Davis, a fellow student, took her to their
holiday place at Lake George, New York, overwhelmed her with
kindness and then "put up a tent for me to write in and nobody
comes near me. . . . I've got my book nearly all done. I like it better
myself now, and do hope I shall get it off this time. I shall have to
type the alterations when I get back to New York."[26] Then later, "My
book is at Macmillan's. I really shall be sick if I don't get it off this
time."[27] This is not yet *The River* but apparently a revision of the
old script, which is not referred to again.[28]

In term time she stayed close by the university, revelling in its
libraries and spacious surroundings, leaving the city for later explor-
ation. She wrote to her sister: "Nothing could describe the adorable-
ness of American women and girls. . . .I really love the life as I've
loved nothing else, altho' I'm dashed hard up. I've very little above
my board and fees left over. But I'll manage somehow." Though she
could do nothing material on her side of these friendships—and in
fact had some need of the restaurant treats and clothes given her—
she was substantial moral support, being strong and uncomplicated,
and always dropping easily into the role of big sister. Esther Norton
Soule remembers her as very reserved on personal matters and "very
uncomplaining. She talked in vigorous, decisive (rather controversial) manner, very positive about her own opinions, but I always
knew she was good-natured underneath this brusque speech. She
rather liked to sound like a Shavian heroine, unsentimental and
harsh, a non-conformist, but she was really very tender. She encouraged me to be a 'modern' woman!—career, suffrage, literary
ambition etc."[29] Jane Mander was very fond also of Mr. and Mrs.
Norton, who thought her so responsible—and in fact she was a few
months older than Dean Gildersleeve—that they allowed Esther to
leave the hostel and set up in an apartment with her in Morningside
Drive; they sent her as chaperone with both daughters to France in
the summer of 1914, and the three were there when war broke out.

In the third year she was ill and let exams go; she had overworked
at supplementary jobs, and there may have been a conflict between

her desire to write and the professional subjects just ahead of her.
There was no point in struggling with these unless she proposed a
career in journalism; accordingly she attended lectures in academic
subjects until 1916, detaching herself gradually. The downtown
art theater movement probably helped draw her from the university: "I was lucky in seeing the beginning of, and in belonging from
the start to four playing groups. . .first the old Washington Square
Players, many of whose members were later to form the now inter-
nationally famous Theatre Guild of New York; the Provincetown
Players, notable as the producers for the first time of most of Eugene
O'Neill and Susan Glaspell, and fourth, a tiny group on Grand
Street, in New York's East Side ghetto."[30] Here was one more liberation: "When I was a girl, people thought it an awful thing to go
to the theatre. Some of them still do."[31] Dates indicate that she was
already wrapped up in the playhouses while she was writing *The
River*.

The need to earn found an interim answer in the women's suffer-
age movement, when Mrs. Carrie Chapman Catt gathered her
forces to concentrate on the New York State referendum of 1915—
to such purpose that it was looked back on as the decisive battle.[32]
Jane Mander went to Trenton Falls for the summer with her land-
lady, Miss Hill, "a great character, with money and schemes,"[33] who
took an old hotel in 250 acres of land to provide cheap, and in some
cases free, holidays for young city girls. Jane was part manager, part
teacher. The *Utica Daily Press* reported enthusiastically on the
Trenton Falls establishment, where Miss Hill and her team offered
free hospitality to visiting suffragettes, and went themselves into
surrounding centers to talk at street corners and deliver pamphlets.
Jane Mander's speeches were featured, her nationality giving her
news value; she took the opportunity of extolling social conditions in
New Zealand, and, speaking with authority from a country where
women's franchise was more than twenty years old, she demolished
fears that having the vote would incite women to rush out to take
office and neglect their children; she instanced the decreasing
death rate among New Zealand children, the "most wonderful labor
laws in the world," and the superior quality of people in public
office as proofs that votes for women brought nothing but good.[34]
The summer ended with a month's campaign tour of the state.
"Father would be scandalised if he knew the street meetings I've
addressed, standing on the proverbial soap-box, or on the seats of

motorcars. . . .I love the street meetings—it's amazing how orderly the crowds are and my voice is an asset. I've one of the best carrying voices in the country. . . .Mrs. Chapman Catt wants me to start in here, and I will do a little. It's like a great political campaign, and is lots of fun."[35]

In the same year she undertook research at Sing Sing for New York's Church of the Messiah. She was greatly taken with Warden Osborne's experimental methods, and she developed a personal concern for some of the prisoners which she kept urging her friends to share. Her next paid employment was with a movement for persuading America to prepare for the coming war; she went on to work for the National Guard Relief Committee and finally to the Red Cross as manager of the New York warehouse where she remained until some time after the end of the war. In 1917 she moved to 117 Waverly Place, off Washington Square, where she shared the top floor of an old house with a friend. She stayed there for the rest of her time in New York and made it the setting of *The Besieging City*.

Meanwhile she had incredibly found time to write *The River* "which I really meant to polish up after the war was over. But through a friend I was persuaded to get out the script and send it to the New York manager of John Lane."[36] He sent it on to London where it was recommended for acceptance by Edward Garnett who told her subsequently that it was the only novel by an unknown writer accepted by the firm that year. The news reached her just before the Armistice, and she at once planned a trip home on the strength of it; but *The River*, promised for the spring lists of 1919, did not appear until early in 1920 in New York, six months later in London, by which time her expectations had made touch again with reality. She was prepared, though, to stake more on her writing, and the loan from good friends of cottages in the nearby countryside enabled her to apply herself with some continuity. But "unfortunately I was wrongly persuaded by Mr. Ralph Block, scenario reader for the Goldwyn Co. in New York, to try to write books that would film. My next two stories, The Passionate Puritan and The Strange Attraction were the results of that misguided venture, a mistake I ever afterwards regretted. With these three books out in both America and England, I went in 1923 to live in London."[37] Before she left New York she had the joy of a visit from her sister Anne, who spent some months nursing at the Presbyterian Hospital. This was the only time in twenty years overseas that Jane Mander saw any member of her family.

II *London*

For the next ten years she worked wholly with books, turning to help other people's through the press as her own output dwindled. Her path to London had been circuitous; now that she was there and forty-five years old, she would lead the literary life that had always been her ambition. London would probably have been her first choice at any stage; as she says in *The Passionate Puritan*:

> No Englishman is capable of feeling for London that concentrated reverence and yearning that comes to the dreaming colonist on a New Zealand hilltop or an Australian plain. To most of these London has the painful lure of the unattainable—the mournfulness of saying year after year "Perhaps I can manage it next," and of fearing the while that it won't be managed. But the illusion is hugged and fed and never allowed to die. There is always the prospect that something may happen—and one may really get there at last.

The comparative peaceableness of *Allen Adair* (1925) may be partly due to the comfort of being in a city soothingly domestic in scope and deeply familiar to the heart.[38]

Though it was not in her to be exclusive, her persona changed now from that of the dashing all-rounder, which life had forced on her, to that of a professional literary woman. Whereas in New York she had earned her living by administrative jobs which were a kind of glorified housekeeping, with only the day's remnants for books, she kept afloat in London by reading and editing for publishers and by freelance journalism. Nothing was very lucrative; her royalties were meager, and Dodd, Mead & Co. of New York had let pass their option on her fourth novel; New Zealand was unappreciative, or worse, and it was plain that she could not be a full-time novelist. Nevertheless, there was nowhere else she would as soon be, though there were pessimistic moments in one of which she urged M. H. Holcroft, who had come from New Zealand to try for a foothold, to go right back home while he still had the price of a boat ticket.

No doubt the long hours with typescripts hastened the attrition of her creative drive, but the worse enemy was the persistent homesickness she could not afford to foster. New Zealand was too distant for a visit, and anything more protracted was unthinkable as its economy had no place for the specialist, its society no tolerance of *métier*. She wrote about her adopted homes when New Zealand failed to respond to *Allen Adair*: *The Besieging City* (1926) is set in New York; *Pins and Pinnacles* (1928), in London. In 1931 she wrote to Pat Lawlor: "I am now in the country for the summer, and hope to take my seventh novel back finished. I am beginning to get very tired of London. . .nearly twenty years in two big cities has made me long for country life, and if I take to that it is back to New Zealand I shall come for it. Indeed, I have a hankering now to get back to my original environment in writing. Apparently no one else will ever be able to do that gum country of the north which is in my blood and bones."[39] According to a letter to her literary agent she submitted the seventh novel, a "doubtful book," to Gollancz late in 1931. She kept the returned script by her, perhaps for some years, but is presumed to have destroyed it without completing the revisions she intended.[40]

An occasional short story or sketch was produced for English papers as Jane Mander's need to earn drew her talent into paths where it could not flourish. More successful were her London correspondent's columns for New Zealand newspapers—articles of substantial comment on plays, books, concerts, and art, besides those of much good sense on general topics—a fair indication, also, of her continuing enjoyment of London's diversity. These satisfactions and her friendships in part counterbalanced the harm done by prolonged city life. But the reckoning is acknowledged in the quotation from E. M. Forster which prefaces *Pins and Pinnacles*, and her handwritten copy of this was left—it could only be intentionally—in her stringently sorted clippings file: "this nomadic civilization which is altering human nature so profoundly. . .and throws upon personal relations a stress greater than they have ever borne before. Under cosmopolitanism, if it comes, we shall receive no help from the earth. Trees and meadows and mountains will only be a spectacle, and the binding force that they once exercised on character must be entrusted to love alone. May love be equal to the task!"

Her renewal came from the company of the talented young, especially those she could help. Derek Patmore has recalled the trouble she took to arrange that he should meet her friend Lloyd Morris whose interest might help his career;[41] Mr. Patmore has since added that "she never complained about her life. She was extraordinarily self-sufficient, and curiously very happy. . . . Her life was well organised: work during the day, and then evenings devoted

to her few friends. She seemed very well aware of what she called
'the apartness of the writer.' Yet she was a vital and amusing companion, and although she never had much money always enter-
tained her friends handsomely. . . .But she was very stern about
herself, and would never spend money she could not afford. Indeed,
she was an enlightened Puritan."[42]

In the later London years she was able to leave routine work for
the absorbing joy of the Harrison of Paris publishing venture. Fi-
nanced by Barbara Harrison and guided by Glenway Wescott and
Monroe Wheeler, the Press set out to issue chosen texts in limited
editions which should be as beautiful as fine typography, paper, and
illustrations could make them. They printed on the Continent for
lower costs and proximity to the requisite skills, but employing
foreign typesetters increased the scope for error. Jane Mander was
responsible for seeing the books through the press; according to Mr.
Monroe Wheeler she loved her battle with the printers and "did a
beautiful job. . . .She was a big girl, with immense gusto—tremendously articulate and exuberant."[43] In their spectacular edition of
Aesop's Fables, kept as close as possible to the Lestrange text of
1692, Jane Mander was responsible also for the textual research and
reveled in it. The strictly utilitarian had always dogged her, even
in the format of her novels, but there for a while she escaped into
fine craftsmanship.

III *New Zealand*

By 1932 her health was low, and in Auckland her mother was in
a final illness; it was time to come home. She stepped ashore in October, too late to see her mother, but just in time to keep house for
her father who was very much alive at eighty-five. There was a
place for her here as a "sheltered daughter," but in finding any
other role she was to meet currents even more strongly against her
than those of twenty years earlier. Her father's need of her was sad
and specific; affection, conscience, and a sense of fairness to sisters
who had carried the home duties during her absence kept her
bound, though often vociferously rebellious. Financially she was
powerless; even if her father had been of a mind to subsidize another
departure, three years of severe depression had so whittled all men's
holdings that anyone not already bankrupt knew he might be any
day. The same conditions bore cruelly on her chances of earning for
herself.

The depression had "settled on New Zealand like a new and un-wanted stranger, a grey and ghastly visitor to the house."[44] Robin Hyde could write from the perspective of 1938 that "its stimulating effect on the thought and culture of rebellious young minds, in a silent country which at last learned to be articulate, was probably worth all the hardship involved. No New Zealand writer regrets the depression." Jane Mander arrived six months after the Auckland riots, into the exhausted, motionless era, and, refusing to accept that there was anything that guts and vision could not remedy, pro-tested when she had time. "One is reminded of the treatment that is occasionally given to new-born babies who have difficulty in breathing," wrote Ngaio Marsh of Jane Mander's series on New Zealand writing in the Christchurch *Press* in 1934. "The infant is seized upon by the mid-wife and accoucheur, violently swung to and fro, submitted to scientific buffetting, tossed up and down, and knowledgably slapped until it draws breath and takes life. Miss Mander's energy tempts one to liken her to a sort of literary mid-wife and to hope that the inert infant may respond with a lusty howl."[45]

Public results were negligible, but privately Jane Mander had sought out the younger writers, who were mostly grouped in a wretched existence around Auckland, to give what succor she could; divergence of aim or style was of no consequence provided they were serious, and she became the friend of almost all of that decade who are known now. "Since my coming to live in my new quarters a lively circle of artists and writers, Jane Mander, Robin Hyde, Frank Sargeson, Roderick Finlayson, Linsay Fraser and Allan Barns Graham and his wife had gathered about the Stronachs," wrote D'Arcy Cresswell in *Present without Leave*, "and on more than one occasion I read aloud to them round the old lady's fireside as much as I had done of *The Forest*, and many times we discussed Mrs. Salter and in what manner the play must conclude." And on another page, "Jane Mander, the novelist, who was now back from London, sometimes placed her house and her hospitality at my dis-posal, besides sending me sums." D'Arcy Cresswell, who was penu-rious then in a primitive hut on the North Shore, added: "I would lie in bed of a night-time reading by lamplight (Jane Mander gave me an oil-lamp for my bedside) while the wind drove the sea into bays and cliffs of the coast and roared through the trees in the darkness around me. . . ."[46]

Another focal point was the short-lived printing press in the university's students' quarters, where Robert Lowry and Ronald Holloway, distinguished young typographers, produced several student publications, the university's Jubilee book, and the four issues of *Phoenix* that made literary history—all now collector's items. Jane Mander found her way there, commissioned a bookplate on hand-made Chinese paper from a wood engraving by Stephen Champ, and steered their way whatever work she could, including any printing needed by the hospital where her sister was matron; similarly if the hospital or her father needed a day's odd-jobbing done she saw that it went to Frank Sargeson, whom Frank Mander came greatly to respect for getting down to it in this manner. When the printers moved from the university to set up in a small way in town she would often turn up to get them a hot lunch, knowing how poorly they ate, but she would never give them copy for pamphlets as others were doing, telling them—and with reason—that what she was then writing was not worth permanence. Her novels had fallen into the limbo; only *The River* was ever asked for, though the Auckland Public Library placed no restriction on the lending of Jane Mander. Proust and Bertrand Russell were less privileged: the "Reserved" shelves were crowded these days with standard authors the exploring young thought they ought to read, a word in the ear of a city councilor being enough to banish a book.

"How very trying to be back in that queer and antiquated atmosphere," an English friend wrote to her. "Do you smoke up the chimney?"[47] The university's women students were in fact still fruitlessly petitioning the Professorial Board for the right to smoke in their own common room; but the cigarette was Jane Mander's panache, not to be hidden up any chimney. The place for a gesture was Milne and Choyce's Tudor Room where all Auckland went to see who was setting what tone—a furtive business all around among women brought up to believe that "She got herself looked at" was the ultimate condemnation. Some mild literary gentlemen who took Jane Mander to lunch there found all eyes turned to their table when she used a chickenbone to emphasize a point—what point, they have forgotten. A bookish Aucklander asked to recall what she said at a lecture he chaired has confessed to remembering only his embarrassment at her short skirt.

She still loved to walk—long distances with long strides—a lean figure with blazing blue eyes and white Eton-cropped hair, hurrying forward with a purpose and an authority enough in themselves to bring notice in those unconfident days. "I both liked and admired her. She was ill, angry and unsocial—frustrated, desperate for someone of her own mental calibre," recalls a friend in the Auckland Public Library where Jane Mander used to beg a little back room to finish her articles. "She had no inhibitions. What she felt she expressed. Beautiful clean cut face and head, sharp and full of attack. Like a seagull—her voice too was harsh and complaining. A bird left behind when the flock migrated?"[48]

Under the surface her strength was used up; nothing could come of the brave resolves made to reporters as she came ashore, that she would write more books, would revisit England. In 1934 she wrote to John A. Lee:

Thank you for suggesting that I should set to work again. I'm beginning to feel myself that I'm sort of blaspheming the holy ghost loafing along as I'm doing. But I did need a different orientation altogether. If I do start again it will be in a very different spirit from that of my London life. Nobody who wants to create should ever live in "the swim" of a big city. You simply do not possess your own mind unless you get away from cults, cliques, circles and all that disintegrating influence. It has done my mind good to come back here, even though I have sadly lacked stimulus. . . .[49]

She regularly reviewed books, mainly fiction, first for the *Mirror* from 1934 to 1937, then for *Monocle* in 1938 and 1939— spacious, wise articles, well organized but often quite roughly phrased.[50] She read and advised on manuscripts and addressed clubs and radio audiences when asked, but her concern for writing was used most forcefully behind the scenes where it was most needed, as unwavering encouragement for the few who were seriously applying themselves. Her grip on such friends was strong and undemanding, and with it went a singular capacity for reinforcing their belief in what they were trying to do. Most of her time and energy, however, was quite powerfully drained at home. In 1937 Robin Hyde wrote to J. H. E. Schroder, "Jane Mander is holidaying in a tent up north, trying to escape from the haunting thought of her father who will play bridge with her. . . ."[51]

A growing demand for *The River*, long out of print, encouraged her to arrange for another edition, and in 1938 the local press was able to atone a little for its reception of the first issue. Her father was perilously ill this year, cared for at home by two nurses as well as his daughters. "Now I shall have to find a retired nurse to be a housekeeper and take care of him. I cannot get on with the book of reminiscences I want to get finished for Centenary year. I shall have to take a room in town to work in. . . ."[52] This she managed for a few months, living in Alfred Street alongside the university and going back to her father at weekends, but she had a serious breakdown before any writing was accomplished. Frank Mander's helpless misery shattered her; his countering strength had always been the measure of her own. He died in his Remuera home in August, 1942.

For some months afterward she was ill. Then she moved to a small apartment in Waimea Road, Remuera, which she made memorably beautiful and ran superbly. Her eyesight would no longer serve her for extensive reading or reviewing; her main pleasure was to entertain friends in one of the few places that had ever been entirely her own. She maintained this life for three years against failing health, then arranged with her cousin Horace Kerr of Whangarei to have an easier place built in that town, where she would be near her brother and youngest sister. As she was about to move she suffered a stroke and lived as an invalid in Whangarei; for long intervals she was unable to read, write, or listen to music. Yet notes written to literary friends in this last period show the old warm, practical interest and a strong hand. She died in Whangarei on December 20, 1949.

CHAPTER 2

Clearing the Bush

T HE setting of *The River* is an obscure arm of Kaipara Harbor where Jane Mander lived for about three years before she was twelve. The knowledge and beliefs acquired in the ensuing years, as well as all that her imagination as a novelist invited her to declare about people, are related here to the physical environment she had known in that period of childhood when the senses etch their sharpest record for adult memory. Asia, the child of the story, embodying as she does the author's recollection, serves as the bridge between the literal truth of the scene and the superimposed fictional elements.[1]

In the opening chapters Tom Roland has just undertaken a bush-felling contract at Pukekaroro where he is joined by his British wife Alice with their two little children and eight-year-old Asia, who is Alice's daughter of an overseas marriage. David Bruce, who ferries them up the river, is an English remittance man, a doctor, and Tom's chief assistant. Having snubbed David at the outset, Alice faces virtual isolation in her new home, where her nearest neighbor is three miles away. During an absence of Roland's David attends Alice while she is unconscious in premature labor. Her anger and embarrassment at being beholden to him prolong her illness until he forces her to talk things out; her aversion to him becomes dependence, then love. They finally acknowledge mutual love but remain loyal to Tom.

In Book II a gale and a flood threaten to break the booms which hold the logs in the river; when the fight to save them is over, David goes off on one of his periodic drinking bouts. Tom faces financial disaster, tries to poison himself, and is nursed back to health by Alice and David, who wonder at themselves not letting him simply die. In Book III Asia is eighteen and bent on leaving Pukekaroro, feeling justified now that Tom is prosperous and the children older. Alice stonily opposes her, but David and their neighbor Mrs. Brayton encourage her, and Alice feels betrayed by them too when Asia goes.

Asia does well away from home but returns to nurse her mother through another illness. Two young Australians come to Pukekaroro in Book IV; Asia falls in love with one of them, Allen Ross, who is unhappily married without hope of release. David knows that Asia and Allen plan to live together discreetly and tries to persuade Alice to accept this; she cannot, and in justifying her refusal confesses to David that she had not been married to Asia's father; the bitter results of her own mistake have been the basis of her self-torment and her fears for her daughter. David urges her to let Asia go without comment all the same, and she does. Tom tells David and Alice that he has known for a long time of their feeling for each other and has assumed them to be lovers; without rancor he offers to let Alice divorce him. She will not accept this, and the three prepare to continue indefinitely as they have been, but Tom is soon killed, bringing down a load of logs which he has to wreck to avoid children playing on the line. Alice and David leave Pukekaroro to marry and live in Auckland.

I   *The Arrival*

The setting of *The River* and the author's inside knowledge of bush-felling give it standing as a documentary, and her promotion of Alice and of the various emancipations she stands for suggests that sociological fervor was one of the spurs that drove her through the writing. Her beliefs, motives, and affections, however, combine in the creation of characters who transcend the immediate limits of time and region. The novel's stature and its permanent claim lie in the viability of Alice and Tom Roland, and to a lesser extent in Asia.

The book is uneven: the author gives too much background explanation, both scenic and sociological which is unfused with her characters and less able than the dialogue. It has a first novel's excesses of too much material and too many words. Jane Mander wrote to a friend on its reissue in 1938, "I should hate to have to review the River myself, for its crudities would hit me in the eye now."[2] To another, she wrote, "Parts of it read as if I'd been trying to show off—and I suppose I was. Too much of reading Bernard Shaw and Nietzsche. And I was too enthusiastic about social movements—the bogus and fuzzy ones—without waiting to see how they'd affect the future. But I wanted to write about normal human beings—not all the funnies and eccentrics. It's more difficult to make ordinary human beings convincing."[3] The irrelevant features of

The River, what Katherine Mansfield called its "false wrappings,"[4] do obstruct, but they can be let fall away to show the undistorted image of ordinary people. At the outset at least the author is true to her underlying intention; she rings up the curtain briskly on characters who are much less remarkable than the surroundings they are trying to come to terms with:

"Damnation! I wish they would hurry up." David Bruce stamped his numbed feet upon one of the few reliable planks in the landing-stage, which threatened to collapse under his vigour, and blew upon his hands, rough and contracted by the cold. The only person within hearing, Sonny Shoreman, a lanky youth whose manhood was not yet under way, hung shivering over the side of the black punt that was moored to the rotting piles of the little wharf.

Alice and her children are on the scene within minutes; by the end of the chapter they are all with Tom Roland in their home at the other end of this tidal river. The characters of the principals are declared and the tensions which will propel them through the story are wound up while we look, in the space of the long day and evening of the opening twenty pages.

The first meeting between David and Alice goes wildly wrong—a usual enough device in introducing two people who are to fall in love, but used here ingeniously for multiple purposes. David has spent the previous night drinking and has not bothered to tidy himself up; when he sees that Alice has more class than he expected he curses himself for his carelessness. "As Alice turned her grey, day-of-judgment eyes upon him, with a look that instantly judged him and dismissed him from her consciousness, he realized how much she resented being formally introduced to him as an equal." Asia stepping forward to be friendly is at once drawn off by her mother. Next, as David and Sonny row desperately to keep ahead of the tide, their dinghy towing the punt the family sits in with all their possessions, including Alice's piano, she tells Asia not to stare at the men. Asia asks whether they don't get tired and Alice says "No, they are used to it." She is wrestling with the graver implications of the journey:

Every mile of it meant a mile farther from even such limited civilization as she had left behind. . . . It was just eight o'clock now, and they were to go on like this hour after hour, until two, or perhaps three in the afternoon.

. . . Once, as she turned, Bruce saw the expression on her face. All sense of hurt left him as he realized that she was horribly afraid.

By rising above hurt David soon attains the godlike position he keeps for the rest of the story, while Alice cements herself into her awkward one, by being unable to thank him naturally when he jumps into the river to pull Asia out, and by failing to consider whether the rowers have anything to eat. When Alice discovers David's quality, which she does soon enough, the embarrassment lasts for months; she is stuck with her mistake among a handful of people who all think the world of him, and in this end of nowhere she has journeyed to there is no hiding anything. Jane Mander's prolonged use of the agony of embarrassment through the next chapters is masterly. As an emotion it is at once the proof of a fixed code of proprieties and an index of the code it grows out of—essential to any convincing novel about New Zealand, where the air has always been stiff with it.

They come at the end of the day to where Tom waits for them on the beach, near the house he is building them. "When the punt finally grounded against the shells there were no signs of eager greetings on either side, but only an obvious 'Well, you're here' from the boss and a composed acquiescence from his wife." The house is rough and small, looking "just about as hopeless and as near the end of everything as it could." Asia thinks it is marvelous. Alice works at putting things in place, settling the children, then prepares a meal. "They all sat down, and the boss began to carve the chicken as if he were charging an enemy. All through the meal he dispensed what hospitality there was with a flourish, showed himself absolutely ignorant of the subtleties of social intercourse, excluded Alice from the conversation by talking fast to Bruce of timber measurements, sucked chicken bones with audible approval, whistled when he was not talking . . . ." David does his best to civilize the meal by including her; she cannot or will not respond. "Immediately after the meal, to Alice's dismay, they started to weatherboard the kitchen."

She goes to sit outside, to rest and cry, until David leaves and Tom calls her to bed. "She knew that he would not consider the fact that she was tired to death. She knew he would simply feel injured because her vitality was not equal to his own. And she knew that if, later on, the children woke up and cried she would have to get up

and look after them, and that he would blame her for the disturbance. In his eyes she would not be equal to her job."

II *The Microcosm*

One page and one week later a new character is introduced as a
solvent, the principals being now too set in their unease with each
other to be able to communicate. Mrs. Brayton, their English settler neighbor, walks over the hill in shot silk, carrying a tortoise-shell
card case, a bunch of violets, and "Mrs. Humphry Ward's latest,
and a wonderful new novel called *The Story of an African Farm*,
by an Olive Schreiner, new writer to me." Age, wealth, and breeding give Mrs. Brayton an advantage over everyone else in the district; she makes touch with the Rolands individually, becoming a
loving mentor and confidant to each. In the education of Alice she
amounts to a pressure course, treating this formal call as a first
lesson.

"Do you read French?" asked Mrs. Brayton, laying the books on the
table.
"Yes."
"That's good. Do you know Voltaire?"
"No."
"Now, don't say you're a Puritan," said the old lady, who had guessed
she was.
"I'm afraid I am rather," answered Alice doubtfully.
"Then you must be cured. Puritanism is an awful disease. You must read
Voltaire. I consider him as valuable as the Bible. I shouldn't like to face the
world without him. Are you a churchwoman?" To Mrs. Brayton there was
only one "Church."
"No, I am not," replied Alice uncomfortably.
"Not a Wesleyan, I hope," in obvious alarm.
Alice laughed suddenly, her whole face lighting up. Mrs. Brayton thought
it was a pity she did not laugh oftener.
"No, I am a Presbyterian."
"Oh, that's all right," with great relief. "It's a state church anyway, and
they do educate their parsons."

Mrs. Brayton suspects that Alice has been "putting on airs with
poor David":

"Let me tell you he is a gentleman. He is one of the few people I invite
to dinner. . . . And when we English people find ourselves away in places

like this we can't afford to snub each other because of a difference in the work we do. . . . When I met David Bruce first he was digging gum, but when I found he read Voltaire and played the violin. . . . I am a chattering old woman. . . . Don't be offended."

Stimulated by having a newcomer to size up and instruct, Mrs. Brayton runs on through this visit and the Rolands' return call; the conversations realistically imitate the standard maneuvers of British immigrants meeting for the first time, their practiced sounding of social strata which both reveals and determines their attitudes. Sitting at an English tea brought in by English servants in Mrs. Brayton's sumptuous house, Alice is recommended to read Oscar Wilde and cultivate a modern intellect, to let the children go barefoot,[5] and to refrain from trying to dominate her daughter. She is meek under these horrifying propositions, because Mrs. Brayton, as her social superior in terms of their homeland, represents the only class who could possibly persuade her to rearrange her notions of propriety. Mrs. Brayton's philosophy is one that Asia will try to build her life on, but Alice cannot effectively alter herself in time to accept that spontaneously.

By the end of the third chapter Jane Mander has so diversified the points of interaction between the principals of her small cast that she has created a microcosm of the New Zealand society she knew. Mrs. Brayton can say to Alice "and remember when you are inclined to feel blue that, whatever happens, you will have an Englishwoman, and . . . an Englishman to see you through," establishing between herself, Alice, and David an unshakable expatriate solidarity. She is in New Zealand only because her son insisted on coming; she has no liking for the local scene as such, and she says to Alice of Tom, "He's one of the few colonials I thoroughly admire." But her genuine interest in people leads her to accept affinity and character wherever she finds them, going to the heart of the matter with the free-ranging courage of judgment which grows only at the upper and lower extremes of Britain's stratified society. She will have an alliance with the strongly colonial aspect of Asia, while Alice, who goes by the labels she has been taught, condemns herself to be part of the inflexible middle of the new country.

One of the opportunities offered Alice with her change of environment is intimacy with such a woman as Mrs. Brayton whom she would have been cut off from at home. The author has endowed Alice with enough formal education to meet Mrs. Brayton on roughly the same level of discourse, thus exposing the vital question: whether Alice can pick up enough mental style to discriminate between the proprieties that are tied to human values and the ones that are only tribal customs. Jane Mander could not have troubled as she did to make Alice her most profound study if she had not seen her as the embodiment of stultifying attitudes which were a waste —even a negation—of the new country's possibilities.

The shakeup of Alice in Mrs. Brayton's house gives us the first of the too few closeup views of Tom Roland. Alice has just played the *Appassionata* and the *Pathétique* to Mrs. Brayton, and they hear whistling in the garden:

Alice was annoyed that he should arrive at that moment. Then she realised that he had been asked to dinner several times, on his own merits, before he could possibly have gained any glory by exhibiting her as his wife. And he had dared to whistle familiarly to announce his approach through that garden.

Tom Roland entered boisterously, a hurricane of vitality. The Venuses and Apollos seemed to sway as he passed.

"Well," said Mrs. Brayton gaily, "how's the bush?"

"Oh, pretty good. Tramway's begun. Soon you'll see the logs coming like greased lightning down that slope to the bay. Things'll hum, I tell you."

"I'm sure they will," she laughed, sitting down quickly, lest he should do so first, and be a fresh cause of humiliation to his too-observant wife.

In his rough tweed suit, hardly clean, he dropped into a tapestry chair, his reddish head against a background of "The Winged Victory." He stretched out his legs, and beat a tattoo on the chair arms, his green eyes roving.

"My dear," said Mrs. Brayton to Alice, with a twinkle in her eye, "your husband has turned us all upside down. Men from the gum-fields and boys from the farms are all flocking to his standard. He's a born leader. But he is wasted here. He should have been in the army."

Tom Roland laughed shortly.

"Oh, she don't appreciate me. She ain't interested in the bush."

"Well, she has never seen one.[6] I was not interested till you took me through those wonderful trees that day. And you know I think you are a vile Vandal for cutting them down."

"Pooh! If you thought of things like that you'd never do anything."

"Quite true. The race is not to the delicate. It's to the ruthless and the strong."

"Don't know anything about that. But I do know that if you are a ninny you never get anywhere, and you never get anything done." He poked a finger into one ear, and tapped with his feet upon the carpet.

Mrs. Brayton laughed.

Alice, who had moved into a low chair, sat back watching them. In that incredible afternoon this seemed the most incredible thing of all.

III   *The Mother*

Granted that *The River* has many strengths outside the character of Alice—there is Tom Roland for instance, certain aspects of Asia, and the reality of the river community itself—each reading confirms Alice's stature in relation to the whole. Professor Joan Stevens regards Jane Mander's choice of setting as deliberate in that it is "vital to the inner experience which she attempts to express. It is the stage on which the heroine works out her personal salvation, the dock for her trial by ordeal." As a puritan, limited by the Victorian teachings of her girlhood, Alice is "unable to make any kind of spontaneous outgiving of personality; she is only half alive. The little river community is most effectively chosen as the place where she can be taught the meaning of love and of life."

This, it seems to me, is what *The Story* is really about, Alice's rebirth as a thinking, independent, generous woman capable of response. Note how she enters upon her stage on page one, being towed up the river by Bruce, the remittance doctor who is to be the chief agent in her awakening. Immediately she has to face the brooding dominance of the natural world, typified by the bush, and the insistent claims of personal relationships from which she has previously sheltered behind class barriers. The frontier society begins to break down her taboos from the moment of her arrival.

Only incidentally during the story do we see Alice outside this world, until, having lived the new life to the full and learnt its lessons, she returns once more down the river, this time with Bruce beside her. Within the microcosm thus contrived, Alice Roland becomes a true person.[7]

It is tenable that Jane Mander began the novel autobiographically —as the story of Asia growing up in Pukekaroro, then leaving it to complete herself—but that as she wrote the forces of opposition gathered themselves together in Alice.[8] In the novel Asia meets discouragement only in her mother; everyone else abets her except Tom, who remains neutral. This is quite a long way from autobiography; Jane Mander's father was opposition indeed, even if her mother made her feel more of a brute. The father of real life is turned into a stepfather in the novel and put into the wings; Jane Mander's siblings, close to her in age, are reduced to infant half-siblings. Every mutation clears the stage for the girl's confrontation of the adversary; but the girl loves the adversary too much to find victory in conquest or flight or in anything but changing her so that they can go forward amicably together. Therefore the story must be the account of the adversary's change of heart.

To any native New Zealander born before about 1935 Alice is a very familiar figure; to the majority of Protestant New Zealanders of this vintage she is the older woman who has shaped them. Alice is, of course, an extreme case; as Dorrie Harding says in *The River*, "Oh, I know there are excuses for her. But lots of us have had a Puritan upbringing and we are not as bad as she is." Many New Zealanders who have been luckier in their mothers find that Alice has been there among their aunts, their schoolteachers, and the best friends' mothers who must be placated. The type could perpetuate itself for generations because part of its belief was that families should keep to themselves, which could be managed well enough behind the drawn blinds of suburban streets. Numerically strong, no other type could so properly stand as the generic mother of New Zealand—or for New Zealand itself as seen by one of its daughters. The figure has courage, rectitude, endurance, and a formidable capacity for work. It is short on some of the traditional virtues of the maternal figure—warmth, amplitude, compassion, and inner certainty. When perplexed it clips a few wings, including its own.

IV   *The Daughter*

Asia, the intelligent, impulsive, and very credible child, captures scene after scene in the opening chapters, as if to announce the reign of the young in New Zealand stories. "If childhood themes appear too often, it is not because they are asked for, it is simply because they are too well written to be rejected," the editor of the *New Zealand Listener* wrote of that journal's short stories as late as 1961.[9] The best writing in *The River* runs parallel with Asia's early girlhood; from her teens on it becomes diffuse and argumentative. Jane Mander did not feature a child elsewhere except lightly in *Allen Adair*, where Joan is present rather as her father's consolation than as a principal, and episodically in *The Passionate Puritan* and *The Strange Attraction*.

Asia's responses are as fresh as the scene she steps into, dignified also by the certainty that she is as special a person to others as she is to herself. Of strong body and unclouded disposition, she offers continually to Alice a cheerful view of the people and situations they face. The little rough, isolated shack that is Alice's despair is opportunity, even ecstasy, to the child who can see herself helping to make it home. In the Asia of the first four chapters Jane Mander has given us the quintessence of her own testament of childhood: she always held that her own had been privileged, and she tried to sweep her compatriots into embracing with equal gratitude their opportunity as colonists. If they let in anything miserable, timorous, or mediocre, they betrayed the occasion.

Tom's kindliness to Asia can surely be attributed to her enjoyment of Pukekaroro. He is irritable with his own children, who are of course too young to be rational and useful; and in his odd appreciation of Asia, so unlike his general indifference to the household, there is some measure of his loneliness. Neither tension nor alliance develops between these two, however, and he takes most of his comfort in dubious ways outside the house.

If Asia as peacemaker to the adults seems to have picked up Cedric Errol's mantle, it is stripped from her soon enough. The first real hurt of her life comes not from anything in the unknown but from her own mother, whose love and trust she had always been sure of. Asia runs home from an outing full of excitement over treasures found in the bush; Alice discovers that she has had an unsuitable boy as companion and thrashes her in a panic. Asia escapes to Mrs. Brayton, and David is able to put matters right by explaining to her that her mother is sick; the reconciliation is easy enough. But through the various strains of Alice's illness Asia grows into accepting without rancor an overresponsible, almost managing position.

The buoyancy of her naturally sane and eager temperament was to triumph later over her present riot of seriousness, but at twelve years old she was prematurely aged by two great emotions. Alice had no idea of the complexity of Asia's outwardly natural devotion to David Bruce, or of the depth of her understanding of her mother's tragedy. She never knew how many nights the child sat up in bed, wretched beyond description at the sounds of Roland's sleeplessness. She had no idea of how much she saw and heard.

But she did see and rejoice in what she would have called the noble qualities of her child: the devotion, the sacrifice, the sense, the usefulness.

She could not have managed without her any more than she could have without Bruce. . . .

The rub comes when Asia is eighteen and wishes to leave Puke-karoro to earn her living; then Alice, opposing her as most mothers of the time would (with the added and still secret reason that she feared for her a downfall like her own), adds a sense of injustice to Asia's normal restlessness. We see that it is innocent of Asia to expect fairness, but the two had been friends once, much more than most. Asia makes ready to go and says to Mrs. Brayton:

"I've never known anything so awful as these last two days. I don't know what has come to Mother. The pater went to the bush yesterday, saying he would not be back for a week. He hates a gloomy atmosphere. Betty and Mabel are scared to death, and even Bunty is subdued. The house is like a *morgue*, and that foolish mother of mine like an avenging angel. All because I want to do a perfectly natural and rational thing. Oh, how is it that human beings can be so silly? . . .

"Oh, I've felt, Granny. But I've felt all I'm going to feel. There's a limit. If she had been different it would have broken me up to go. But she has made me hard. All I want now is to get the beastly business over. What is the matter with Mother, anyway?"

In this farewell evening with Mrs. Brayton, the inevitable moment for stored-up questions, Asia asks her about David and Alice: "Have you ever thought about them—wondered? . . . They must love each other. I'm sure they do; but whether there's ever been anything I can't say. And it's been so easy for them—the pater away such a lot and when I have gone out in the evenings I've said where I was going and how long I'd be away." "Child!" protests Mrs. Brayton; Asia has moved faster than they suspected.

"Well, my home has been the sort of place that one would move in, if one could move at all," replied Asia grimly. "Isn't Mother enough to make you think? And is there anything slow about Tom Roland? . . . Why did Mother stand it? What good does it do to stand things? She never made him any better . . . . Mother has taught me one great lesson. I'm done with misery. I shall have nothing more to do with it as long as I live. I shall train my mind to ignore it. I won't cease to help people, or to be sympathetic, but I'm not going to suffer over anybody any more . . . ."

Asia confesses that she has loved David; that is why she wonders how her mother can resist him. Mrs. Brayton sits up very straight and finds her tongue: "Your mother and David have a rare and beautiful friendship—a spiritual friendship. You have no right to think into it something that is not there just because you feel too deeply." "Look here, Granny . . . here you have been educating me for years to understand unusual situations, and to discriminate, and now, when I apply my knowledge to the facts under my nose, you try to put me in the wrong. . . ." She goes on to speculate aloud about why her mother ever married Tom, and about her own father who "must have been a more joyous soul than Mother, perhaps an awful scamp, and that's why she would never speak about him . . . I'm sure he was a sinner . . . and Mother has never forgiven him. Sin—sin—the word that has hypnotized the world."

Asia is not a lady; Alice has maintained her own gentility somewhat at the expense of the daughter whose enforced capability now gives her the strength to leave home. She is not worried about the future, but she wants her mother's loving approval of her freedom almost as much as she wants the freedom itself. The final hurt is when Alice lets her go with a cold goodbye: "They leaned towards each other, and with averted eyes their cheeks slid past each other, Each felt the other stiffen, hesitate, and harden again, and then Asia was gone out of the door, through the gate, and down the path." Mrs. Brayton manages to break through Alice's "pride and foolish aloofness" and is rewarded by a rare confession: "I do not know what is the matter with me . . . . Feeling makes me blind. It does something to me . . . . I don't know what. I have been cruel to her and it is all my fault. And today I couldn't wave to her. I couldn't— I wanted to, but I couldn't—"

Asia's return to nurse Alice through another illness is an interlude of thaw before her mother ices over again at the interest Asia and Allen show in each other. The daughter now requires her mother to drop the "manner that would freeze hell," to stop thinking what she is thinking, to be hospitable to this young man, and to "act as if you are enjoying it." The novel becomes protracted; Alice is slow to catch up. It is only after her own happiness is secure that she can bring herself to trust in Asia's, and in shepherding her to this point, through the various stages that end in Tom's death, the author keeps the flair which is hers whenever Alice is in question. But Asia is given too much rope in proving her case. Argument and doctrine take over, dating *The River* at the very moment it strives for contemporaneity.

Whatever truce Jane Mander might have made with her own memories of breaking from home as she wrote *The River* at close on forty, the company of young women with wounds still raw precluded pacific treatment of the theme. The students of Columbia University were, moreover, the first group she had been part of; though never quite as isolated as Asia, she had all the same missed the solidarity of a shared viewpoint that comes with long schooling or a fixed home town. The idea that Asia's struggles in the Kaipara are prolonged and intensified out of concern for young women in New York is borne out by the article Jane Mander wrote for the *New Republic* in 1916:

The sheltered daughter is to be found in all kinds of homes where economic pressure has not found its way. She is one of the crimes for which poverty is not responsible. She may be preserved for various ends, of which the three most clearly defined are the marriage market, safety "in the hands of the Lord," and the comfort and use of her parents. . . .

I know I am treading on holy ground. Parents do make sacrifices for their children. They will work for them, they will fight for them, they will starve for them, they will die for them. But they balk at the idea of letting them go off to work, to think, to fight for themselves, the most intelligent of all sacrifice, because the independence would rob them of so much food for their own emotions. . . .

In the last three years, round about Columbia University, in dormitories and apartment houses, from all types of girls, rich and poor, I have heard bitter indictments of parents for the cultivation of this helplessness. "My mother never taught me anything," "My parents made me helpless," and so on; pitiful tales of domination, opposition, selfishness, of the tragedy of many futile attempts at adjustment, of final heart-rending breaks, which only the strong and the courageous could face, all for the right to be self-reliant, to get out and challenge the world.

These cases are all the more tragic when, as often happens, there are people of strength and quality on both sides of the struggle. It is a terrible thing to have to wound the people one loves. Those of us who have gone through it in the fight for personal freedom never quite get over it. Those of us who have turned in the road to look back at the motionless figures in the doorway who have made us feel like murderers when we wanted them to bid us Godspeed as joyous adventurers, who have chilled our enthusiasms so that we feel that we can never turn to them save in pity and tolerance, know that life holds few things sadder. If in the end we can forget the hurts, if we can recover some mutual respect, we have something to be thankful for.[10]

V *The Boss*

"It is a commonplace, of course, that a novelist will sometimes create better than he intends, and this, I think, has happened with Tom Roland," wrote Frank Sargeson. "Miss Mander has intended Bruce and Mrs. Roland to be the most important persons in the story, but Alice's negativism is so extreme that she sometimes comes close to being an unsympathetic character, while Bruce's fault is that he is somewhat too good to be true. But so accurately has Tom been rendered that, almost without the novelist knowing it, as it were, he turns out too true to be altogether good. In other words, he appears before us as a complete man. . . ."[11] Tom Roland persists in seeming a little involuntary, and one of his major appearances—the late scene where he confronts Alice and David—is commended by Katherine Mansfield as a place where the author is "off her guard."[12]

Jane Mander is otherwise very deliberate, firmly guiding the reader to a conclusion, leaving no margin for speculation. Even with the complex Alice, each stroke builds up to a controlled picture. About Tom, however, her mind is divided: she is hard on him because her passionate viewpoint is from within the Roland household where he is nothing but a trial. Every now and then honesty jerks her into seeing other aspects of him: each of the motley crowd of bush workers has a "secret admiration for those men who, being superior, do not parade the fact. Every man in that crowd liked the boss. He worked with them. He ate with them. He swore with them. He was extraordinarily fair with them. He had a way all his own of being familiar, and yet, at the same time, commanding their respect."

Tom has his success with women, too, from Mrs. Brayton's amused admiration to Mrs. Lyman's long devotion of heart and body, besides the passing conquests hinted at. Even domestically there is another way of looking at him, which David puts to Alice:

My dear, you must stop being hostile to him. That is not fair. If your marriage was a mistake, it is just as hard on him as it is on you. . . . Tom is not rough on purpose. Few people are. You feel so badly about Tom's manners that you are apt to overlook his great qualities. You know, we British are too damned superior about our culture and our refinement, too intolerant of differences. We forget that the pioneers and the sons of pioneers made the world possible for us. . . .

Like most of David's wisdom, this comes from such a height of reasonableness as to be unusable; it has nothing to say to the nerves and senses which determine the climate of life in a small house. A person does not have to be at all bad to be quite intolerable close at hand, but the causes and results of irritation are extremely elusive to a novelist; some of the sufferer's animosity may rub off on the author, as it does in the case of Tom Roland, and again when Marion Adair is in question. There is even something excessive in the atonement Jane Mander makes Tom in the end, giving him a hero's death, a lying-in-state and a piling-up of obsequies in which everyone weeps for him—except of course Alice and Asia.

Tom jumps into the book self-propelled—as if through a gap in the author's pros and cons about him—unprocessed by intellect and lit by talent of a different quality from that which infuses Alice and Asia and the major figures of the other novels. The ambivalence is inherent in the "feminine view of the masculine world, which is the chief virtue of the book," as *Tomorrow*'s reviewer wrote, adding: "She, like the female characters she created, never attains that intimacy with primitive physical nature that seems natural only to men. Her outdoor world is but a background to her indoor drama. . . ."[13] It is true that the outside is never as close to us in the author's head-on descriptions of it as when Tom irrupts indoors, trailing its aura as plain as the mud on his boots. He is more part of "primitive physical nature" than any settler could be at that stage—and it is interesting that although settlers were already in these districts they never come right into the novels. Where bush was the enemy, the man locked in combat with it belonged quickly and heroically by his violence, while the settler's acclimatization crept on him as he harvested year by year. The strongest parts of the book are those where the disparate elements are collected under a roof—Tom representing the great outdoors—to fight it out in the limitations of space and scene a little theater would work within.

Such is the peculiar but credible scene that is Tom's last indoor appearance alive. He comes late in the evening to David's hut, finds Alice there being comforted, retreats apologizing, and is summoned back by David who insists on saying "Tom, this looks bad. . . ." David and Alice find he has assumed her unfaithful to him for years; he has been keeping out of their way, making it easy for them. David is appalled that Tom has thought he would so abuse trust. Tom breaks down, saying he had had his chance with Alice and had failed; he owed David a lot and he was more Alice's style. Up to this point the men are concerned primarily with their own friendship, but Tom then turns to Alice and asks whether she wants a divorce—there would be no fuss; Mrs. Lyman would oblige. Does he want to marry Mrs. Lyman? Alice asks.

"Not particularly."

"You have lived with her on and off for years, and you don't want to marry her?" she asked, not understanding.

He mistook the meaning of her tone.

"Well, that ain't remarkable," he snapped. "Lots of men live with women they don't want to marry. Why don't you learn something about the world you're living in? You saints! You don't know what goes on under your nose. I'm no worse than other men. I'm not half as bad as some of them that you've met and been very pleasant to. If you knew more about life you wouldn't condemn me."

"I'm not condemning you," cried Alice passionately, her face set in an effort at control. But she could not help herself. She sat down on the bunk and burst into tears.

"Oh, for God's sake," he exclaimed impatiently. He hated any scenes he did not make himself, and he wondered why on earth they had all got into this.

CHAPTER 3

Society Moves In

T hree more novels of New Zealand life followed *The River*, each based on Jane Mander's direct experience of the frontier society subjugating the landscape and improving itself. Primarily a social observer and diagnostician, she kept up her attack on the "disease of Puritanism" and its equally deadly local concomitant —the materialism of suburbia. By the time New Zealand's hostile neglect obliged her to write of other countries, she had shrewdly and substantially recorded the early manifestation of the very outlook which was to grow sufficiently pervasive by the 1920's to secure the downfall of her published work. Besides contributing quite individually to this general theme, each novel amplifies a separate phase of the early environment. *The Passionate Puritan* (1921) is in part a happy and oddly unquestioning documentary of kauri milling; as such it is the logical starting point for the necessary inquiry into the author's own beliefs about the abrupt removal of these forests. In *The Strange Attraction* (1922) a Kaipara townlet a generation later than *The River*'s community, is busy with the appurtenances of second-stage pioneering: two rival newspapers and a hotly contested parliamentary election in which local grievance is a major issue bring to the surface some of the author's working philosophy of politics. *Allen Adair* (1925) returns to an earlier stage of pioneering, and here the man's world—the gumfield—is threatened by the values of an embryonic, contiguous suburbia. All three novels bear witness to Jane Mander's fervent love for her own part of the north: in *The Passionate Puritan* the love is predominantly that of physical enjoyment, and in *The Strange Attraction* it has a patriotic flavor; *Allen Adair* is her plea for the north's integrity as the stronghold of social freedom and unpretentiousness, while in relation to its landscape she allows her love some tentative steps toward the mystical.

After *The River* Jane Mander never again wrote wholly to her own specifications. Each subsequent novel was shaped, and in some cases even distorted, by various outside influences and expectations she had to reckon with in her determination to become a full-time novelist, preferably a novelist of the New Zealand scene. Chapter 6 gives details of her own country's responses, on which are based the supposition that she wrote *The Strange Attraction* while receiving her initial wounds from this quarter—hence this novel's peculiar disorganisation and bravado—and that *Allen Adair* was placatory because a resilient philosophy enabled her by then to offer compatriot readers a fresh set of proposals for mutual understanding. It is likely, though, that she completed *The Passionate Puritan* before the cold winds from the southern hemisphere reached her; the pressure on her at this point was to make enough money to buy time for writing and to compensate as soon as she could for her late start; *The River*'s long-delayed publication would need to be followed up quickly. Very mistakenly, as she afterwards saw it, she let herself be persuaded to write books that might be filmed.

The Passionate Puritan woos the films with a lightly romantic theme and two long documentary episodes—the tripping of the dams and the bush fire—which are built up to proportions overweighty for a short novel and are more in keeping with the cinema's extended, suspenseful usage. Her urgency shows in the speed with which she dashed off the story: "This book was written in one month, which may explain why it is what it is," runs Jane Mander's inscription in the Alexander Turnbull Library's copy. Yet as a novel it is both felicitous—being the product of still happily confident energy—and very much to the point.

I   *The Scenario*

Sidney Carey, the "passionate Puritan," arrives at Whakapara on her way to the sole charge school at the Puhipuhi mill. At the top of the exam lists, brilliant in the classroom, she is here through the Education Board's ruling that every teacher must serve two years in the country. James Ridgefield, the board's chairman and a personal friend, has secured her for this mill which he owns. Wishing to write, Sidney has accepted a journalist's advice: "You're not half developed, even for your age . . . you've never been in love! And you really don't know the country. . . . By all means go to Puhipuhi. The very thing you need."

The use of a small community to develop a wider response to life

—a pattern that evolves in *The River*—is explicit from the start. "Sidney Carey, at the age of twenty-four, expected great things of herself and of the world. And in this belief she had been encouraged by most of the people she had met in her native city, Auckland." With a "lavish share of objective tendencies" and a "minimum of introspective ones . . . she had sailed through the world with her head up, her eager eyes and mind roving to learn of anything and everything but herself."

Jack Ridgefield, the mill manager, meets her at the station and takes her by timber tram first up the mountain face, then along three rough miles of plateau to the mill settlement. Her acceptance of this way of traveling, to which there is a slow alternative, establishes the mill's dramatic setting and the physical hardihood that characterizes Jane Mander's heroines. The community has built her a cottage, "unpapered, simply lined and ceiled with heart of kauri. . . ." Grateful and proud to have her, they will do everything for her comfort, but their reverence isolates her. "To them she was more than woman, as a minister and doctor are more than man to the small community dependent on them." And the women "knew perfectly well that all talk of their husbands about democracy, and all men being equal in Socialist New Zealand was just rubbish when it came to women. They may have wondered why they were not as good as Miss Carey, but they knew they were not, and that was the end of it." The publicity of her daily life, the excessive importance of her smallest act or remark, form the townswoman's first shock; she soon feels "naked at the top of a post."

Sidney finds the quiet, capable Jack Ridgefield worth considering, but he slips off to town and comes back with a wife. Next she meets Arthur Devereux, an English settler dressed and mounted in county style, who diverts her; she encounters him again when she visits Mana Tamahere, a Maori whom she has already met and found more congenial and better educated than the Pakeha women —a good musician and the owner of books by Wells and Conrad (the year is 1912) as well as of inherited Maori treasures. Mana's husband, an interpreter in the land court, is away much of the time; her liaison with Arthur, which Sidney at once suspects, is on the whole discreet and not too destructively deep. Arthur and Sidney acknowledge their love after a few more meetings, but Arthur is worried about how to break with Mana without hurting her. Sidney overhears the Ridgefields mention that Arthur has a wife in

England; Arthur explains that they have been separated for years
and are arranging a divorce. He finally placates Sidney and coaxes
her to take a less earnest view of life, though she considers that
he has been slippery. She wishes she could respect him as she does
Jack. Arthur then tries to argue her out of chastity, takes her on a
boating holiday in Auckland with other couples less scrupulous,
and breaks her reserve but not her resolve. Later, during an absence
of Arthur's, she is shattered by evidence which she interprets as
proof of his continuing intimacy with Mana. Before she has time
to break off the engagement there is a bush fire to which he returns
to join her in acts of heroism. Only after his own brand of joking
philosophy has slowly persuaded her not to dismiss him does he let
her learn that there is an innocent explanation for what she has
suspected. They drink to his toast: "To monogamy, and may it be
as interesting as it ought to be. The good Lord help us both."

II   *Variations on the Theme*

Because the story is light and quickly written we can observe in
shallow water, as it were, the shape of philosophical conflicts which
are sunk deeper in the other novels. Here the puritanical character,
again a woman, requires liberation from her prison of strict consistency, if it can be managed honorably. In *The River* David says of
Alice, "The devil is she doesn't know how to be inconsistent," and
puts in years altering her; to David mainly, and to Mrs. Brayton in
part, we are invited to give credit for Asia's greater flexibility. Sidney, likewise, is due to be limbered up. Arthur Devereux's role is
to compère the scene for her, to hasten her understanding of the
changes forced on her by community life, and to supplement them
more intimately himself. Conversationally he is very reminiscent
of David, of whom he is a frail, ungodlike, rather naughty version.

The rescuer has to come from overseas; a native New Zealander
could not conceivably manage. The upper-class English are used
in the first two novels, an eccentric Australian in the third; either
will do, in fiction as in fact. By presenting Sidney as already fully
endowed with intelligence, principles, capability, and awareness of
the arts, the author underscores her view of how much still had to be
done for even the finest products of local culture of the day.

To bring in Mana as an already perfected person, a philosopher
on the side of warmth and liberation, is to emphasize further the
puritan's isolation from humanity. Modern New Zealand thought

concerns itself with the puritan Pakeha's need of the Maori's complementary temperamant and values, seeing as self-destroying
the efforts to make the Maori over into his own image. Mana is the
only Maori personality in these novels, which is strange. Jane
Mander grew up in districts where the Maori population was high;
both her brother and her youngest sister married into the race. The
comparative silence of a writer authoritatively close to the theme
now paramount may indicate that she did not see it as a theme in
itself. And indeed between the end of the Maori wars in the 1860's
and the renaissance of the Maori race (which one might put at
about the time of Jane Mander's death) lay a period in which the
matter seemed to rest, at least in the Pakeha mind. It is suggestive,
however, that Jane Mander's only Maori character is deployed as she
is.

Arthur is something of a remittance man, like David Bruce of
The River and Dick Rossiter of *Allen Adair*. His burdens are a di-
sastrous marriage back home and a sense of futility:

> . . .my dear girl, you take my up-bringing—the usual thing, tutors, pub-
> lic school, Oxford, sport, the estate, family, clubs, the Code, and you have
> your machine-made product—me, futile because I am machine-made. Put
> me against a man like Jack Ridgefield, why, I'm pathetic. I'm a pleasant
> nobody. And worse still, I know it. I've never done a big thing in my life. I
> couldn't build anything. I haven't an original idea about life. You think.
> So does Jack Ridgefield. You've both got the courage to change your habits.
> You'd change half of them for a new idea. I wouldn't think any new idea
> was worth changing one of mine for. That's what the system has done for
> me. . . .

As a New Zealander of her time Sidney is too much in love with
England to be put off by this; the representative, the embodiment
of England, need not come in very wonderful human form to be
accepted gladly.

Arthur had made good use of their last meeting. He turned her thoughts
to the future. He painted alluring pictures of England, of trips to the Continent, of London. And she saw how much he looked forward to seeing it
with her, and to having her help him to forget the tragedy that had driven
him from it.

She needed no stimulus to look forward to it. That magic phrase "the
estate" conjured up scenes of rural charm and old-world atmosphere that in
their secret hearts the most democratic of "far-flung" pioneers adore. And

London! No Englishman is capable of feeling for London that concentrated reverence and yearning that come to the dreaming colonist on a New Zealand hilltop. . . .

Sidney's moral reservations about Arthur have to stand up against her picture of herself as his wife, redeeming him and—again in New Zealand fashion—doing more good in another country than in her own. "She was more interested to have him talk of the future, a future in which he meant to take up the responsibilities of his estate. She was eager to contribute ideas for the benefit of tenants, eager to spur him on to benefit the human race. The fact that he had no real work to do had troubled her more than she would have admitted even to herself." She has to acknowledge, on her second break with Arthur, that "since the first renunciation she had added to him a vast number of things that she was to get with him, and how much these things meant to her she had had no idea till now."

III   *The Brother*

This novel's dedication is "To My Brother." The Gillespie Radio Portrait says that "Bill and Mrs. Hardy are disguised only by name. Mana, flattered in the novel, was really a most unwholesome character who lived at Puhipuhi. . . .Jack Ridgefield is her brother. . . ." However good the authority for these identifications, it is dangerous to take them literally. There are some obvious parallels here in that the author's brother was manager at Puhipuhi for his father and in that his engineering inventiveness and his management of a diverse crowd of men were on a par with Jack Ridgefield's. More profitable is the less literal speculation: that in Jack Ridgefield Jane Mander portrayed a capable, sheltering figure whose essence and effect was that of her brother as she had known him. Bert Mander was only seventeen months younger that Jane; at fourteen, according to Port Albert neighbors, he was working with the strength and responsibility of a man. Her own childhood virtuosity would remit nothing to her brother; the family situation could extend any number of capable children. Lacking only their father's restless drive—which was too disruptive at close quarters to be seen as a virtue—her brother could stand as the wholly admirable type evolved by the new country. If she wanted a symbol of what she most loved and admired in the native scene, nobody could serve her better. We have to take Jack Ridgefield with Allen Adair to see roundly the type of man she envisaged as the best product of the country she had to reject for herself.

Sidney's divided mind is worth scrutiny. Arthur says to her: "My dear, you're half in love with Jack. He's the alternative to me. You'll always be liable to turn from my type to his type. If you don't know it now you will some day." Sidney finds herself "astonished and disturbed by his insight." Even after Jack's marriage and her commitment to Arthur, Sidney "would have liked the chance to try her personality on him, would have liked to get at him. She saw that Arthur was a transparent babe beside him." Jack at the same time found "she now interested him because she had shown that she could do good work. Because she had managed to keep her independence and yet offend no one in the village. Because she had a conscience and character. . . .But he did not understand her in the least. If men were simple to him, women were inscrutable mysteries. He was more or less at sea with her mentality and always would be. He was extraordinarily pure male. And he got near women only through the medium of sex."

Though Sidney is the most normal and nubile of Jane Mander's heroines, she decides against the New Zealander. The fictional selves of the New Zealand novels—Asia, Sidney, and Valerie—are ambitious, academically gifted, world-minded, full of zest for moving away from their origins. The brother men are peaceable, fulfilling themselves in service to a small community. This novel contains their most direct confrontation; the brother image is missing from *The River*, and *The Strange Attraction*'s Valerie has mentally disposed of Bob Lorrimer before the story begins, though he stays around. But between Sidney and Jack marriage looks so natural and desirable that each must secretly consider it; each comes respectfully to another conclusion. This may be Jane Mander's apologia for her own decision against New Zealand.

IV   *The Suburb in the Bush*

Just as Sidney lets into her reckoning about Arthur "the things that she was to get with him," the author lets us see what a woman would get with Jack. The theme of self-inflicted standardization is introduced for the first time in this book, repeated as a commentary in the next novel, then used integrally in the person of Marion Adair. Sidney finds the village "almost a perfect specimen of bourgeois respectability" where "Not a woman in that place dared to have a front room suite of furniture that differed essentially from anyone else's." She had expected to find "raw human material" in the bush settlement, and "treasures of native wit."

But the village was too prosperous. Everybody in it was saving money. And the women especially reflected the influence of growing bank accounts. They had evolved from the crude state that produces native philosophers into the state of "getting on in the world" wherein philosophers rapidly perish and die. . . .There was no Irish "drunk" to delight Sidney's heart, no cockney charwoman to take the world with vivid humour.

On her part Sidney is "too clearsighted to be satisfied only with comfort. And though she despised the idea of being an example in the ordinary sense, she was not without her notions of the mission of the teacher." But the children are dull and docile, the product of overcareful parents; she thinks longingly of the terrible Auckland class of sixty boys who had started each day determined to get the better of her. Worst of all was the realization that she would never change anyone's ideas. "She saw that she had only to suggest a new way of doing a familiar thing, such as bottling tomatoes, and everybody in the place would at least have tried it. But if she had suggested a new way of thinking about God as force, or sin as defective education, they could not have followed her an inch." By the end of six weeks she is hating their smug prosperity. Jack Ridgefield brings his new wife from town, and "Before she saw her Sidney was sorry for Sophie Ridgefield. She felt she was doomed to an even greater isolation than herself. She foresaw that Jack would want to keep his wife apart from the gossip and pettiness of the village, and that probably she and Mrs. Jack would now constitute a little aristocracy of their own. . . ."

In *The Passionate Puritan* we are nearly three decades away from the first-stage pioneering of *The River*: Puhipuhi is accessible and comfortable enough to give its people a margin for personal development. Jane Mander's anguish at the opportunity wasted, at the brave new world stultifying itself, begins to sound through her novels, to be taken up by her in person when she returned to New Zealand.

V   *"Lawfully and in Good Faith"*

The state-owned Puhipuhi forest of 17,000 acres had been ravaged by fires in the 1880's, losing a third of its area and 300 million superficial feet of timber. Some allege that gumdiggers fired it, in despair at their exclusion from the forest; others that bushmen wanted the immediate employment of salvaging timber from the partially burnt larger trees. Jobs were very scarce in those years. Cutting went on by lessees, of whom Frank Mander was one of the last, like the Ridgefields of *The Passionate Puritan*, taking on the less accessible high country areas. As usual only the most rewarding trees were taken, the land then being totally cleared for farming, though land that suits the kauri makes most reluctant pasture.

The Mander family's milling experience reached a bold climax at Puhipuhi, though long before they were there the forest was being boosted as a tourist attraction: "the most easy of access from Auckland for visitors who desire to see the industry in full work. Here the tree is being felled, cross-cut, hauled to the mill, cut into boards and shipped to the railway. The whole modus operandi can be followed just as conveniently as you can see a pig driven into the Chicago Slaughter Yards, and presently produced as sausages at the other end of the factory. A main road, the Air Line, runs right through the Puhipuhi, and the visitor can either walk or ride."[1]

In usable bulk the kauri is the largest timber tree in the world; the Australian gums are taller, the sequoia thicker and taller on the average, but neither of them carry the thickness up like the kauri, whose trunks will run up to a hundred feet before the first branch. It dominated the northern part of the Auckland Province, interspersed with other and almost equally valuable timber trees. The individual settler, away from milling facilities, simply got the trees out by fire and ax as quickly as he could, in desperate need of pasture. Industrial city people, for the most part, with no tradition in caring for the land, were forced to fight it out unequally, without the technique for partial conservation, even if they had had the education for it. The whole bush covering, the growth of centuries, was treated as the crop of a season. In 1919 a timber expert wrote supporting the opinion that "the cost of this war to New Zealand would have been paid for had the original Kauri forests of the Dominion been worked and preserved as are forests in most civilised countries, and this could have been done with a considerable gain in the amount of timber available for cutting, and some gain in permanent land settlement."[2]

The state, too, cashed in quickly on any timber it owned, for the government of the day was always in need of money for its own programs, which in some cases were the costly ones of liberal humanitarianism. The odd voice protested. William Pember Reeves, for instance, spoke of

the great area deliberately cut and burned to make way for grass. Here the defender of tree-life is faced with a more difficult problem. The men who are doing the melancholy work of destruction are also doing the work of colonisation. As a class they are, perhaps, the most interesting and deserving in colonial life. They are acting lawfully and in good faith. Yet the result is a hewing down and sweeping away of beauty, compared with which the conquests of the Goths and Vandals were conservative processes. . . .the work of our race in New Zealand seems more akin to that of the Seljuk Turks in Asia Minor, when they swept away population, buildings, and agriculture, the Byzantine city and rural life together, in order to turn whole provinces into pasture for their sheep. [3]

But the prevailing viewpoint was the one expressed by Frank Mander in the House in 1905 when he said that the way to provide for the future was to plant "suitable trees, for it was no use trying to preserve colonial timber." He did not see why it should be preserved: "it was like coal in the earth—it was there to be used." He was in no sense politically powerful—merely the agent of the community's will, having about the same influence as a colonel in the army.

His daughter, by contrast, was uncomfortably placed as a writer, being looked to as time went on for a philosophical solution, the more so as her novels do have their platforms. Conservation is not one of them, though *The River* admits bush-felling to be questioned—from the womanly, esthetic viewpoint, which the realities of the case at once expose as sentimental. Alice and Mrs. Brayton are being conducted to where Tom's gang is cutting kauris.

With a catch of her breath Alice saw, towering up out of the green depths on either side of that open way, row upon row of colossal grey pillars. . . .

"There!" Roland put down the luncheon baskets he was carrying, and waved his hand airily at them. "Best bit of bush in the colony. Nothing to beat it outside of California. Those trees have stood there thousands of years. Might have stood there thousands more."

"And you are going to cut them down!" exclaimed Alice as if it were sacrilege.

"You bet I am. Great job too. Takes some tackling. . . ."

"I've told you what I think about it," said Mrs. Brayton.

"Rot!" laughed Tom. "What would you have people live in in this country? Timber is cheaper than bricks. These trees make houses for the poor. Somebody has to cut 'em down. Look at the people who can own their own houses in New Zealand. Why? Cheap land, cheap timber. Something you don't have in England. And you talk sentiment to me! Pooh! Come on."

They stand well back to watch a tree that is to come down; the axes are finished, the wedges in, the whistle goes for the men to stand clear, but "there was not yet a quiver in all the dark mass of foliage, no sign of capitulation to the wanton needs of man. Straight as the course of a falling stone the slaty grey trunk shot up seventy feet without a knot. Nothing could seem more triumphantly secure." Then the tree quivers, the sky line wavers; Tom calls "She's coming."

The whole world seemed to lurch, slowly, slowly; then the top branches shook, the great trunk swayed, the foundations cracked. . . .it plunged forward, filling the whole visible world, and cracking horribly, till its longest branches caught the ground with a series of tearing, ripping sounds, preliminary to the resounding roar as the massive trunk struck and rebounded and rolled upon the earth. . . .

"There, that's over," said the boss cheerfully. "I guess we can have lunch now. . . ." He could not understand why Alice had tears in her eyes.

Other troubles claim Alice's tears from then on. Her long reverie that same evening traverses her own unhappy state, the disturbance David has added, and then dwells on the compensations: her children and Mrs. Brayton, her books and her music. "And there was her husband. She knew now that he was a power in the land. He would make money, and perhaps he really meant to do his best for her and the children." Mrs. Brayton, moreover, who dubs Tom a "vile Vandal" for cutting the kauris, is living comfortably on land very recently brought in from the kauri forest. Later David persuades Alice to accept farm produce from the Braytons on credit saying, "There's no charity in it. Tom's plans will make Brayton. The township here will mean better roads, a bigger local market, increased price of land . . . doubled and trebled prosperity for every one who lives here. And no one knows it better than the Braytons. . . ."

This is as close as Jane Mander comes in her novels to questioning the physical processes of colonization which surrounded her childhood; in this respect, at least, she appears to see her elders as they saw themselves, acting "lawfully and in good faith" and, moreover, hounded by necessity. Outside her novels she made one significant reference to the bush:

> We had our skyscrapers in those days, but they were trees; trees that walled off the rest of the world and held up the sky. They were also our antiques. I thought of them as old as God. My first sense of terror, of rage at the ruin of beauty, came from seeing them cut down to make homes for the invading settlers.[4]

As the bush was vanquished corporeally, it returned to haunt literature. The farming that supervened was modern, plunderous, and unlovable. By the time Jane Mander returned to New Zealand there were younger writers preoccupied with what had been done. M. H. Holcroft wrote:

> In New Zealand the artists are bound to accept, consciously or unconsciously, a responsibility incurred by our people when they first came to these islands. Do we think often enough of the manner of our coming, and of what was done here in the early years of settlement? D'Arcy Cresswell has written of the "great shout of progress" which arose while our ancestors were occupying the land. It was a time of hard work, of clearing and burning, of destruction and building. The colonists came into the country and possessed it. We see today the results of their activity—prosperous cities, farms and factories, roads and railways, and all the signs of comfortable living. But we see also the bare hillsides, the remnants of forest, the flooding rivers, and in some districts the impoverished soil. The balance of nature has been changed. Are we to assume that a people which possessed the land in this manner—raping it in the name of progress—can remain untroubled and secure in occupation? Is there not something still to be done?[5]

The new ambivalence toward pioneers showed up in some reviews of the 1938 edition of *The River*. To Frank Sargeson, for instance, *The River* described the ruin of our resources with a power "no modern sociological writer can deny. . . .The land in many places now is little better than a desert. And what have we got in return? Certainly one is unable to find a very satisfactory answer by walking along a city street and using one's eyes."[6]

Jane Mander also thought poorly of what she saw in the same city streets. She upbraided Aucklanders for want of style, mental timidity, esthetic insensitivity, and interminable cake-making, seeing all this as a betrayal of the wonderful start New Zealand had been given by the enlightened men who had pioneered its education and legislation. Sanguine by temperament and brought up in the era of unlimited hope, she always tended to believe that the present could put anything right if it made the effort. There is no sign that she wished the past different; and indeed to reappraise the past would have been cataclysmic. If the New Zealanders she had most admired were her brother and men like him, the matter lay too deep to be shifted.

It was not as if the country had evolved other types to which she might have been tempted to transfer admiration, nor was it in her to write a novel of disillusion. She was a little stranded, as a gallant colonel's daughter might be among friends who had reached the conclusion that the whole war had been a mistake. This may have been a factor in her long silence from 1932 onward, though at what level of consciousness we cannot tell. *The Passionate Puritan*'s picture of bush-felling is quite unclouded; we are invited to admire the techniques, the men who operate them, and Sidney's physical enjoyment of the scene. The queries are social, applied to the values the village lives by.

VI *"Cheaper than Bricks"*

The notable documentary section of *The Passionate Puritan* is the account of the tripping of the dams. James Ridgefield has come from Auckland with a party of friends and tourists who wait with horses and vehicles at the big dam for Jack, who is "working his way up the fifteen miles of creek from the mill, tripping dam after dam as he came." The Big Dam, the showpiece, was easily the largest in New Zealand, having taken twelve months to build. "It was a quarter of a mile across, fifty feet high in the bed of the creek, and backed up a temporary narrow lake two miles long, and in places half a mile wide."

This lake, now a jam of logs, containing four million feet of timber, seemed to take up the whole of the valley in which it lay. Leading through the bush, over the ridges all round it were the wooden tramways and roads that fed it.

The valley itself was picturesque in a ragged desolate sort of way. It had been swept by fire many times, and was mostly a graveyard of skeleton trees. Everywhere the fern and scrub had rapidly covered up the ashes.

Jack rides up with his team, joins the gang of bush workers carrying long spiked poles; after introductions, orders, explanations, he and his men "went onto a footbridge that ran the whole way across the top, the latter going right over while he and Bob stayed above the gate. Workers who had been poling logs into the centre of the lake now made their way back to the shore, jumping from log to log, and giving a final push to the one they landed from."

It was a clear morning, and the valley was very still. There was no sound of bush work, for every man had been taken off to stand by the creek to prevent jams at the numerous bends all the way down to the mill. . . .

Suddenly the clear air was cut by the exciting sounds of horns blowing a series of signals far down the gullies. The echoes ran round and died away. And then there rang out one long clear call, followed by three short ones. . . .

Jack Ridgefield turned on the footbridge, gave one look to see that no man was left on the logs, called to the men and was answered, and then waved his hand at his father with a funny little dramatic sweep very unlike him.

"Away she goes," he called.

The watchers stiffened. They saw him lean down, pick up a rope and pull it.

And there was no more peace in the valley that day.

On the lower side the great gate heaved up over the first rush of water that was churned instantly to foam upon the rocks. In a minute the dry creek became a raging torrent, filling the valley with its roar. Then in the dam there was created an enormous suction that drew in the logs from all sides. They came slowly at first, till caught by the undertow they rose up like prehistoric water monsters coming up to breathe. They stood on end, poised for a fraction of a minute, and then they dived head first down at the foundations of the dam, hitting the gate upwards with a deafening boom that echoed round the hills. Clearing the gate they leapt up out of the water below it, thundered back upon the rocks, staggered, were swept onwards, hoisted one upon another and swirled off again in a torture of movements that it worried the eye to follow. To the boom of the logs hitting the gate was now added an extraordinary thud, thud, thud, as they bounded from the rocks in the bed of the creek on their mad way to the mill.

The dam will take all day to empty. The visitors watch for ten minutes, then move on to see the logs passing other points on their way to the mill—in many cases to get ahead of them. "The creek wound so that it was possible to leave the Big Dam half an hour after it had been tripped, and by following a straight track to beat the logs to the second dam, to watch them go through it, and so on most of the way down." They ride fast over ridges and gullies, to wait above a dry creek bed.

In a few minutes they felt rather than heard a peculiar beating on the air, a pulsing something, vibrating like the panting of a fast advancing monster. Then they distinguished a dull roar with a distinct intermittent booming in it. . . .

Now they began to see things heaving up and down among the trees above the bend. Above the roar and the booming they heard the churning of the water on the rocks.

All at once, on round the bend it came, a dirty frothing wave ten to twelve feet high, sweeping over the banks on either side, levelling the fern, and on the crest of it, swirled as if they were matches, tossed the tangle of logs. The water came on like a wall. One could have run a yard or two ahead of it without being wet.

James Ridgefield tells them there is a place half a mile ahead where they can see the logs go over a seventy foot fall, but they will have to run for it, and since the going will be rough, he advises a rest.

But laughing they all set off like a lot of children to follow him. It was rough underfoot, but otherwise the track was open. Now and again they could hear the logs booming their way down the creek ahead of them. Then they would lose the sound and pick it up somewhere behind. And so it zig-zagged about them as they scrambled on. . . .

Sidney had been a good runner in her childhood. The race intoxicated her, and did not tire her at all. It added to her excitement to know that Arthur kept looking at her as they ran. . . .

The great crescendo was bursting the valley again. . . . With their eyes fixed on the smooth rocks at the top of the fall they waited breathlessly. All at once the wall of water heaved up into the sky, curled and rushed downwards. The logs, turning somersaults, leapt clear of it. Some of them dived head first into the pool to shoot up later or be smothered under others coming down. Some among the first fell flat with an enormous splash. In a torment of motion they were swirled round till the current caught them and carried them off once more down the creek.

They lunch and wait for the horses, the flood not diminishing during that hour. They move on now past the lower dams where the logs are sweeping through the current.

They rode now to the accompaniment of continuous sound, for the waters of the first tripping had long since reached the mill, and were creating a thunderous outside fall over the overflow and down the ravine.

Sidney and Arthur rode mostly in companionable silence. They found each other easy from the beginning.

At intervals he told her facts of the day's work, that Jack expected to get between four and five million feet of timber down, that when it was over the logs would lie in an unbroken line up the bed of the creek for four miles, that it would take small trippings to bring the stragglers on, but that this combined flood would carry the mill for months, and that by such a system the place was independent of the weather. It had taken Jack and his father three years to work it out, he said. The older man had told what he wanted, and the son had seen that it was done.

VII   *The Townlet*

The story of the *Strange Attraction* (1922) runs contemporaneously with that of *The Passionate Puritan*. The setting now is Dargaville, a town of twelve hundred people, on a broad stretch of the Kaipara's largest river, the Wairoa. As the center of a complex of navigable waters, Dargaville had grown through handling waterborne logs from inner areas long after its own immediate bush was removed. Therefore, without leaving the 1911-14 era, Jane Mander is able to transfer her study of society from a temporary village in the virgin bush to the relative sophistication of the clearing.

Valerie Carr, daughter of "the cleverest lawyer in Auckland," arrives in Dargaville to help on a triweekly paper edited by her childhood friend Bob Lorrimer, son of the Bishop of Auckland. She settles in at the local pub, knows how to make herself acceptable to its mixed characters, and shines at her job. Brushing off the overtures of local society, she relaxes by playing the piano and walking; she is noticed by Dane Barrington from Australia, a brilliant writer with an ambiguous matrimonial past, who lives in a romantic old house outside the township with a collection of oriental treasures and two Chinese servants. Valerie has admired his writing for years; their mutual attraction is inevitable. The newspaper successfully promotes Roger Benton's election to Parliament against the sitting member who is of Ward's Liberal government, and once that crisis is over Dane prevails upon Valerie to marry him. She maintains that she would prefer a lover and a career to a husband and children, but she will live with him if he will keep their marriage secret in the meantime.

Valerie's father visits Dargaville suddenly, having heard of her involvement, and tries to end it by offering a trip overseas. She is explosive and bitter toward him, telling him that his own yachting cronies had destroyed her innocence long ago. Shattered and humbled by her attack, he goes away when she tells him she is already married to Dane. The unaccustomed frankness of this interview has put father and daughter on a better footing. She is able to accept the money he sends as a wedding gift and, with this behind her, leaves the paper and begins to write a novel in the idyllic surroundings Dane provides. Dane is, however, too deeply damaged a person to find the stability he had hoped for with her. Their union is jeopardized by his increasing moodiness, by his return to drugtaking, and, one suspects, by Valerie's restless immaturity. Tragedy saves them from slow disintegration: just before the outbreak of war Dane finds he has the inoperable cancer he has suspected. He dismisses her from their partnership, withholding the true reason, thus freeing her to go away to the war.

This is the second of the two novels Jane Mander wrote with one eye on the films. It is certainly an awkward book—the least successful of her New Zealand novels—though its weaknesses are not obviously related to her divided aim. The chapters that read best as fiction are the very ones that ask to be filmed; conversely, the arguments and soul-searchings of Valerie and Dane, which weary the reader in the later chapters, cannot be seen as coming into their own on the screen. The flaw is rather in the structure: what begins as the story of a community, or at least of a promising assortment of people, narrows to the relationship of two lovers living in unworldly isolation. All Jane Mander's heroines receive a measure of indulgence, but Valerie is the extreme case; she insists that the reader run off with her down one path leaving all the rest of the cast behind. It is possible that this is where the screen influenced Jane Mander, who was no moviegoer and might have thought that the prime requisite was a spectacular part for an actress.

In spite of its imperfections, the book contains much that is enjoyable, illuminating, and just. It is a sharply truthful picture of an emerging northern town; Dargaville's immediate surroundings, their untidiness and aridity, brought from Jane Mander a wryly exasperated style that was her response to defects in places she felt she belonged to—a blend of chastisement and caress that stops well short of satire. Like many other New Zealanders, she appears to have suspected satire as an oversophisticated, even dishonorable weapon for her own use; she could revel in the satire produced by other countries, but her campaigns would proceed by frontal attack. The early chapters also give a quite hilarious picture of small town journalism-cum-job-printing of the era when New Zealand had more newspapers than ever before or since.

But social protest—social awareness—is the real theme, which Valerie's obstreperousness must not be allowed to distort or to shout down. Bob Lorrimer and Valerie have both taken themselves from Auckland—with 100,000 people the relatively big city—and from its privileged set. In Dargaville, the frontier town, they find a rudimentary society shaping itself into the stiff conventions of the one they had left. Bob does not mind much, for he is an accommodating person, a good small-town man like Jack Ridgefield and Allen Adair. Valerie, however, behaves very badly on her first visit to the five beach cottages where the élite spend their holiday huddled in a row, with the whole wilderness around them inviting them to jump clear of one another, at least in their spare time.

Here is brief, trenchant treatment of the theme that runs blandly through *The Passionate Puritan* and poignantly in *Allen Adair*. In Dargaville the reckoning is inescapable and bitter; Pukekaroro of *The River* is not far up the harbor, a reminder of the hopeful stage of settlement. (Dane and Valerie slip up there by launch to be married by David Bruce who has returned as justice of the peace and supervisor of the late Tom Roland's enterprises.) Dargaville, then, is what it all comes to. After one glance at its society, Valerie treats the town only as a place of work and a base for excursions into the surrounding wilds, a line Dane has already taken. They are alike in seeing happiness possible in their retreat well outside Dargaville, or in Sydney in another country, but in no society in between.

Valerie, we are told, "had as extraordinary a patience with disagreeable facts as she had an extraordinary impatience with disagreeable ideas." Jane Mander might be describing herself. Her attack here is only on some of Dargaville's ideas; the purely functional makeshifts—the uncomfortable pub, the unsealed road, the jim-crack printing press—she tolerates, even cherishes. These are inevitable to the situation; they are matters of money, which will come in time, and her values are never tied to money. Nevertheless when Valerie shows a disposition to revel in austerity for its own sake, Jane Mander scents puritanism and calls up the sybaritic Australian to set her right. Over a campfire tea Valerie says to Dane:

"Ah, give me this any day before your satin couch civilisation."

"You think you despise the satin couches, don't you? But what you really despise is the fact that they have been over-emphasised."

"But I do despise them. I love the primitive for its own sake. The satin couch world is cluttered up with such a lot of unessentials, such a lot of meaningless stuff."

"There is meaning at the back of it. But the meaning has been obscured or perverted. You are the product of satin couches, even if you are a reaction against them. You would not appreciate this tent if you had not been brought up on satin. The primitive is fine for the nerves but it is not stimulating to the modern mind. The caveman had a strong stomach but a poor imagination. It takes supremely sophisticated people to perceive the beauty of the simple life. No plebian gumdigger sees the picturesqueness of the nikau whare. It's the man who comes from marble halls who does that. I can write inspired articles about the bush, but the man born in it can't. It's really because you had your grandparents that you love this. So don't despise that background."

Valerie strikes her attitude in the first chapter by answering good-natured Bob's hopes that she will like Dargaville with "I don't care a cuss if I don't. I shall stay till I've got all I can out of it." Later when he questions her propriety she tells him that "If only we would all let each other go pleasantly to hell the world could be quite a nice place to live in." These ungainly pronouncements are a quite genuine cry of desperation from a girl who is not sure she is even now clear of the repressive forces of her relatives and their Auckland circle. The devoted Bob who is part of her past is exposed to her defensive snapping; she does not trust him not to have avuncular concern for her conduct, and she is right. But she is very pleasant to anyone who looks like an underdog and as good as gold when her energies are extended by the election campaign or a printing crisis. Auckland society has pressed her into the most feminine mold of the day, the colonial approximation of the London débutante, when she obviously needs a strenuous career.

The author has not sufficiently built up the background that has caused Valerie's truculence, leaving the past to Valerie to recount as grievance in a manner that defeats its object. The book's misfortune is that Valerie antagonizes readers, though she is a consistent and credible study, with a point of view well worth a central place. But the author has let the control slip, like a mother who takes out

a spoiled child, sees clearly how badly it is behaving, and is too tired
to subdue it. There are no illusions in Dane's summing up of
Valerie:

And then she was much too sure of herself. She was inclined to overrate her
accomplishment in this matter of herself versus the world, to discount the
support she had received from certain factors in her life. She had had, and
always would have in her own country, the loyalty of her class whether she
wanted it or not, and the power of money to shut mouths. She had never
had the poverty that forces one to hunt for bread against prejudice. She had
had added to the force of her own personality, the glamour of her set, despise it as she might.

The assertive front of this very egotistical careerist comes surely
from long hunger for approval which has now reached an angry
despair where she will settle for an adverse reaction rather than
none. One has only to go back to Asia's partings with her mother
and to the "Sheltered Daughters" article to recognize the depth of
Jane Mander's belief that it is not enough to go one's own way—a
blessing must go with it, or the figure on the porch is left in the
unworthy misery of possessive love, and the one who leaves is for-
lorn.[7] Hence Valerie's bravado and her "all let each other go pleasantly to hell," the travesty of to love and to let go. She cannot afford
to grow fond of the town's society because that would give it power
to hurt her by its opinion—an opinion so inevitable as to justify
her feminism:

As far as Dargaville was concerned, Valerie's marriage to Dane did not
cause anything like the talk her staying on the paper afterwards aroused.
It was strange that certain feminist claims were almost unheard of in the
country that boasted the most advanced legislation in the world for women.
A married woman who had struck disaster in her husband or her financial
affairs could, of course, earn her own living with the understanding and
blessing of the community. But that a bride of established position should
wish to do so was carrying the theory of independence a little farther than
it had so far been carried, even in that land.

Although Valerie is an unpersuasive proponent of some of Jane
Mander's causes, particularly of those relating to personal fulfill-
ment, it is otherwise when she forgets her ego in the realities of an
election campaign; here at last she seems capable of empathy. Other
characters also have their say at this point, developing the most

comprehensive picture the author has left of her own probable attitudes to patriotism and politics.

VIII *The Patriot*

The practice of giving even the smallest places their real names ran Jane Mander into trouble with New Zealand readers who built curious superstructures of literal identification upon them. Her successors usually took care to put fictitious names to their places, however exactly they might describe them. *The Strange Attraction* goes beyond real place names into the parliamentary election of 1911; mentions Ward and Massey, the party leaders, by their real names; give pseudonyms to the local candidates; and telescopes into one day's voting a change of government which in reality took months to come about. It makes the dramatic election night the story needs; in perspective it is the historical truth about New Zealand's moment of change between two exceptionally long governments, showing also that the author felt free to leave the literal truth as soon as she had left her starting point—a conclusion we should apply in interpreting her other novels where the literal truth is too private to be known. She appears anxious to prevent her Roger Benton being identified as J. G. Coates who was returned there in 1911; by putting Dargaville in the next electorate, by omitting the second ballot and Coates's nonalignment, notable features of his election, she tells the north that she does not mean Coates. These shuffling devices, required of a small country's unfortunate novelist, are confusing only if the novel is seen as a history text, which would have horrified the author. She is intent solely on the essentials of the north's swing to Massey.

To the modern reader there is incongruity in the sight of Valerie, the fictional self, and the other principals campaigning for W. F. Massey, the stodgy, prejudiced figure who appropriately presided over the early 1920's—the era of stagnation and self-inflicted limitation Jane Mander shot her published novels into. This, however, is to project back the later image of Massey which she did not stay around to collect, having taken herself off to Columbia's expansive teachings a few days before he became prime minister. The Massey of her day was the new man.

She had been able to work editorially on the *Northern Advocate* owned by her father, a Massey man, without noticeable outrage to all her principles. The Liberal party had been in since she was a child; what it had done that she approved of was long done, and hope rather than gratitude determines political allegiance, if indeed any gratitude could survive the daily reminders in the north of what the Liberal party had not done. In mud up to the knees, or on anguished, slithering horses, or in little boats stuck in the mangroves waiting for the tide, they thought of the roads and railways Wellington had provided for the rest of the country. They knew themselves to be on the receiving end of snobbery too; the outburst in *Allen Adair* does not exaggerate:

But the north was not respectable. It was the land of lost men. It was peopled with nomads and wasters. And it was the "roadless north," the "barbaric north," where Maoris still might war upon you in the night. It had no railway beyond Helensville. The southerner curled his lip at it. It had no gold, no coal, no minerals of any kind. It was poor land. Rivers? Harbours? Yes. And the bush? Oh, yes, the bush. But no *land*.[8]

There was enough genuine underprivilege to give her a cause, and one in which she could go some distance with her father. Her zeal was always humanitarian rather than doctrinaire; the north itself was reluctant to wear party labels.

Dane Barrington of *The Strange Attraction* asks Roger Benton, "What is your war cry? Justice for the North?" "Yes, and it's the best we could have. It's high time the Government paid some attention to us. Seddon never did, and neither has Ward. They have lived for the South. . . ." And Benton's pamphlet "above all called to the northerner to get attention for the land he had made his own." Massey was a small farmer from near Auckland, the nearest the north had seen a party leader come to its own likeness. W. J. Gardner has said of his party that "If it had a symbolic figure, it was the bush settler at the end of a mud road—a North Island figure, and a new pioneer, not an old one."[9]

Jane Mander was constant to her belief in change and to her concern for the neglected. Outside that, "I stand aloof from movements and politics as such, and refuse to be regimented into anything, being as fierce an individualist as T. E. Lawrence. . . ."[10] In *The Strange Attraction* the Liberal party "crumbled before that mysterious force in the world that brings about change." Twenty-five years later the old age of the government she let Valerie cheer in had made a different line of demarcation between the neglected and the cared for; she could then very consistently write to John A. Lee:

"Honestly hope you and your crowd will do something to stir up the dry bones of this country. I have even persuaded my old father, conservative all his days, to keep an open mind about you. I have always been on the side of the young, the new idea and the underdog, though perhaps I have not done very much about it."[11] And Valerie by the 1930's, if she had wanted to shock her Remuera circle, would have needed only to cross the tracks in Auckland and campaign for John A. Lee in his city electorate.

Reviewing the 1938 reissue of *The River*, Frank Sargeson suggested that "had Miss Mander been writing today some of us might expect her to tell us a little less about the occupants of the boss' house on the hill, and a little more about the occupants of the men's houses down by the mill."[12] Does not such an expectation, however mild, imply that our emphases of the 1930's can be postulated to the early Kaipara? For the significant part of *The River* "the Boss" lives in a kind of shack that Katherine Mansfield's father might conceivably have put his gardener in, if it had not been on a roadless point, a journey of days from a city. Vis-à-vis the comparatively privileged south, the northerners could often enough see themselves as all in the mud together.

This regionalism—it can scarcely be called parochialism—is no more than compassion for that part of the earth which is small enough to be loved as home. It is amazing how strong a national entity already existed in New Zealand, in spite of the divisions made by the country's sharp, tangled mountains and rough coast. About three days of ferocious travel lay between Frank Mander's electorate and Parliament in Wellington. Yet uniform laws and education, applied to a populace of sufficiently homogeneous background, welded the country in spirit before transport united them in reality, and when Jane Mander made statements overseas it never occurred to her to speak for less than the whole of her land.

IX *Suburb versus Sanctuary*

No two of Jane Mander's novels are in such fundamental contrast as her third and fourth. *The Strange Attraction*—inept, peculiar, and strident—was followed in 1925 by *Allen Adair*, the mellowest and most endearing of all her stories. It is a transition from battle cry to rural ode. *Allen Adair* is the only novel where the author gives a man the center of the stage, and he is one, moreover, whose temperament must find salvation in nonintellectual spheres. Clear of speech-making and progressive ideas, the writing is spare, like the plants of the gumfield setting; the short words and short sentences total a piece that is brief for what it contains.

Allen Adair is the unambitious son of an Auckland lawyer, who sends him at some sacrifice to Oxford in a desperate attempt to make something of him. After two years Allen asks to be excused and returns to New Zealand, where he fails first as a cadet on a Hawke's Bay sheep run, then as clerk in an Auckland merchant's office. Written off by his family, he goes to Dargaville where he is quickly employed running a small mail-and-supply boat to isolated settlers. Soon he is ready to set up for himself and is pushed to a decision by advances from a settler's wife, a practiced siren, from whom he flees to Auckland (where he reinstates himself to a degree with the family), then to Pahi, further up the Kaipara. Here Peter Horton and Jack Asbury, partners in timber-milling, ask him to set up an inland store to serve their bushmen's camp and the adjoining gumfield, which he finds ideal. Wishing to be married, he chooses rather quickly a good-natured girl he has met in Auckland. Outwardly they prosper, but Marion is limited; disappointment grows in both of them over the years until their life together is an armed truce with a good front presented to the world. Allen and Jack Asbury's wife, Geraldine, permit no expression of the strong attraction they have for each other.

Allen takes on the lease of the gumfield, and among the diggers is Dick Rossiter, an educated Englishman, who gives every appearance of being in hiding. As Dick becomes sure that Allen is safe and incurious, he admits him to a friendship in which Allen finds increasing comfort as his home grows uncongenial. Dick is finally free to come out of hiding when a man in England confesses to the crime he had taken the blame for; he then goes home. Allen's success has won over his father, whose death now leaves him quite wealthy. The Hortons and Asburys are pulling out of Pahi; Marion has long desired to move to Auckland; Allen is left with no valid excuse for staying. He gives in quietly, joins as partner and kauri gum specialist the firm where he had once failed, plans to visit Dick in England, and wryly accepts a feeling of futility.

In time the story stretches from the 1870's (given as the period when Allen was at grammar school) to the Boer War. The gumfield and Allen's store are given as lying seven miles inland from Pahi, and there is gum country there; but no point in the district conforms literally to all the author's specifications. She may have scrambled the locality to avoid giving offence and hurt, all too well aware by now of the New Zealand passion for literal identification of places and persons. The story is abundantly true to the district.[13]

X *Men without Women*

Quasideserts created by the kauri forests before the country was inhabited at all, the gumfields lay among areas of forest in full health; they ran for miles alongside the bush in *The River*, and bush adjoins the gumfield of *Allen Adair*. The diggers were casuals of all kinds, from men on the run and born vagrants to nearby settlers whose farms were not yet paying; each made a rough hut, did for himself, and met others only when he went out to trade. Here vagrancy was inoffensive; a man could hole up for a while to work things out or be a nobody without censure. Science has lately found a way of converting this land to pasture, and the country may be as much poorer for this socially as it is visually.

To Jane Mander these areas meant every bit as much as the contiguous bush. She placed a long gumfield episode not very appositely in *The River* and had Dane Barrington of *The Strange Attraction* disappear into the gumfields to emerge with the best stories he had ever written. Her London homesickness focused on them, and they were to be the setting of the novel written after her return to New Zealand. The first exposition is in *The River* when Asia takes Allen Ross with her to visit a dying digger:

All Ross could see as he now looked at it for the first time was a wide area of what looked like nothingness in comparison with the view elsewhere. Its pigmy slopes and valleys, visible by day, now merged into the dead level of monotonous wastes. What vagrant trees it had were dwarfed to the level of the ti-tree and the fern, themselves the poorest of their kind, for the blood of the soil had gone centuries before into the life of the kauri forest, of which now the only trace was the gum, the hardened sap of the great trees that had once proudly whispered to the sun and the stars.

But as Ross looked at it there grew into it the colours he had heard Asia speak about. Such gullies as it had deepened into the strong barbaric blues that the modern artist has rediscovered for the world. Its burnt slopes sprang into life in patches of purple and brown that seemed lit from within. For five minutes its colours stayed hot and crude, like jewels glowing over a furnace, and then a film crept out of the night and dulled them, like clouds of grey tulle spread over a gay and many coloured robe. As they faded out they left the wastes they had glorified more desolate than ever.

Thus *The River* proffers the visual beauty of the gumfield for immediate acceptance, much as Asia Roland is putting it before the
young Australian as they walk it together at that point of love when
much will depend on his first response to it. The long chapter goes
on to become a treatise on gumfields, a chart of their sociology and
ecology which may have cleared the way for the succinct treatment
in *Allen Adair*, and might be taken as this book's documentary
preface.

Allen Adair himself moves obliquely toward his gumfield, which
is only part of his demesne as storekeeper and, at this stage, the need
of only a small part of his nature. He is absorbed first in domesti-
cating himself quite normally, with some of Jane Mander's primary
belief in settlement, her enthusiasm for the people who move in on
the landscape and convert it to their purpose. He tells himself that
it is "absurd that he should be so pleased with himself. It was nothing to be starting a little country store." But he could not help seeing
it as more than that, as

part of an exciting procession of events in the transmutation of bush land
into prosperous farms, of isolation into settlement, of lonely tracks into
railway lines. Already he saw the train of the future speeding along these
northern gullies. Already he saw the cream factories which men down south
were dreaming of as part of every township. And he believed in the thing
that was going on about him. It was all rather vague in his mind . . . but it
was there . . . a justification of his love for the gumfield.

The visual aspect of the gumfield is slow to take hold of him. He
has dreamed too romantically, and riding out to it the first time with
a sense of ritual he feels let down. "It was a place to be lived with by
night and day, by sun and rain, and not merely glanced upon. . . .
Nothing had budded upon its niggardly soil. The stunted manuka
was brown, the crawling lycopodium was brown, the very fern had a
rusted look . . . . The earth had borne too well and was shrivelled
now in permanent exhaustion." But his mind is held by what he
cannot see: the treasure under the grayish pipeclay land and "the
solitary huts from which the outcast men came forth with spade and
spear to dig for the amber gum." These men—"their lives and their
thoughts and their pasts"—made up for him "the fascination of the
place."

To give these men a fair deal and the unsociable security they need becomes the purpose of his life, intensifying as his wife's company becomes less to his taste. When the men of the neighborhood are asked to look over the field for a youth wanted by the police, he turns aside from a clue because he has come upon it accidentally, by intrusion as he feels. He can even put his philosophy into words to soothe Dick Rossiter: "I'm glad you sheltered the kid. . . . I have an idea about my field. I like to think it is a sanctuary, and as far as I am concerned it is." Then, over practical help, "You don't have to thank me for anything. But I wish you'd feel—well, that you are in my house when you are on my field, and that anything I can do. . . ." But this is only to Dick who already trusts him; absence of speech is the only safe way to the diggers' confidence, and Allen is very good at this.

He sets about winning their trust with a patient subtlety which men in some other civilizations might put into courtship. He had not needed art in winning Marion; in fact, his main reason for choosing her, if it can be called choice, is that he had had no idea how to approach anyone less accessible. Two contrasting themes are thus contained within one outwardly simple character, growing and contending with each other: his field and his marriage, the spheres of his adequacy and of his failure. Or if we take Allen as a study in benevolence, we see kindness fortified by intelligence and application becoming effective as kindness to one set of dependents, and goodwill toward his wife having ultimately the effect of cruelty because no such effort of imagination goes with it. Where the gum field is in question, Allen's tact is infallible.

He had now a dozen customers off the field, but in his ramblings he had never yet come upon a hut or a shanty. It was almost as if they came out of the ground like moles. He was happy enough wandering over the dips and ridges. . . . Unexpectedly he met a man with a spade and spear. "Good day," he said, as he dipped down into the gully. "Good day," said the other, emerging out of it. And in five minutes they were a quarter of a mile apart. Allen had recognised him as one of his first customers.

Such a man might come from any background, for any reason; it is this range of human possibility that intrigues Allen, but only as a matter for pipe-smoking speculation. He is no journalist.

A little later he saw a hut almost the colour of the scrub down below him. It was made of nikau, sacking and rough boards. Some flannel shirts and

dungarees were drying on the fern. There was a spring down there, one of
the many that dotted the field and started little streams out to the tidal river.
A man came out and sat down on a box in the sun. Allen turned back on his
track and veered off in another direction.

His triumph is the friendship of Dick Rossiter whose nervy evasive-
ness calls out his most protective quietness. He lets no interest show
when Dick turns up first at night to trade valuable carved gum.
Later, on mail day:

Allen began to put his mail out on the counter. As he lifted out the largest
that Dick had ever had in the country Allen knew that the stranger's eyes
were turned towards him more than once in a scrutiny quick and intense.
But as far as his own manner was concerned he might have been handing
out such mails every day for years.

Dick goes off wondering "fearfully if the storeman would be curious
about him."

All that mail, and then that money for the gum. Certainly the brutes up
north had robbed him on that former lot. But what a godsend! If only the
storeman was as casual as he appeared to be! Flynn had said he was a rare
chap. . . . And to get a store and a post office without a gossiping woman.
That was luck too.

Allen turns on Marion for being curious about Dick's mail, banishes
her from the store, and later tells her that "You women haven't got
the code of honour men have about these things." He is astounded
at his anger. "Heavens above, he thought, why am I going on like
this? He felt he wanted to smash something. He tramped out into
the back garden and up and down between the lines of climbing
beans. Really he must do something with himself."
    Allen lives more and more in an outside room to which the diggers
have access; later he spends two or three nights a week with Dick
in his hut on the field, but will not mention this to Marion, even
when she suspects him of worse. " 'Where do you go then?' 'That
is my affair, but it is not to any woman.' 'How do you expect me to
believe you?' 'Well, then, you don't believe me. Now what do you
want?' " The crisis comes when Dick's name is cleared and his story
breaks in a newspaper. Marion reads it with excitement to Allen,
who takes it from her to read the story he has never heard from
Dick. Marion says: "You might tell me something. I suppose you've

known him all along." Allen says only: "He's the *woman* you've
been so suspicious about," and rides straight across the field to find
him. But Dick has gone, summoned to Auckland by his lawyer. If
he comes back it will not be to live on the field, and without Dick
Allen does not wish to stay in the place himself.

He stood on there a prey to weariness and depression by the place that had
been a sanctuary to his friend and to his own friendship, all now ruthlessly
torn from him. He felt with some concern how much this man had meant to
him, how much he had flavoured the gumfield with romance, how much
he had cared for those two evenings a week when he and Dick made a world
of complete peace for themselves. If Dick was gone he did not care whether
he went to live in town or not.

The symbolism of the gumfield as the peaceable man's private
world is reinforced by Allen's normality, by the degree to which the
author has kept him above the grosser misfortunes and idiosyncrasies that are most men's reason for being there. His route to it has
been that of a mild person backing away from intrusive pressures.
Playing truant from school, "all he had to say for himself was that
he had gone fishing off Parnell Point with some other boys, what
boys he did not know." On the matter of being sent to Oxford he
knows he would have preferred Africa, India—anywhere else—and
ashamed, wondering if there is something the matter with him,
realizes that "his most exalted moments were spent out of doors
where the trees did not press round him demanding to know what he
meant to do with his life, and the sea did not rise up and call him
slacker, and the stars did not drop words of unkind criticism upon
his head." At the sheep station he hated the boss's home, the
mothering women of the house, the long evenings with the family.
Then in the Auckland office, the period of maximum pressure,
when he is failing in the last reputable occupation open to him, a
trader comes in and talks of the north. Allen then knows that "the
north had been at the back of his mind all the time. A free place
where men walked about and picked up gum, or just poked in the
earth for it, and found enough in two days to keep them for a week.
And where you made your own house, and lived as you pleased, and
nobody ever came near you." Knowing where and what the ideal is
gives him courage to go forward, thus breaking with society, because "to go north was a confession of failure. When you could not
get on anywhere else, or if you had disgraced yourself you went

north to drop out without meeting the accusing eyes of your friends. This was the city and the southern point of view."

Allen finds, though, that the solitude and status of running the Kaipara mail boat remove his desperation. He comes to Pahi self-confident enough to take over the gumfield as patron, keeping it inviolate for others. It is only when the pressures of his marriage bear on him intolerably that he has to make it his own refuge. He can protect the diggers from Marion's curiosity and cheap judgments, but he cannot protect himself.

XI *The Encroacher*

Marion, who epitomizes the forces that threaten the sanctuary, enters the story as a fresh-faced, affectionate girl, hard-working and anxious to please. Her intrusiveness, as Allen sees it, begins on their wedding night, when she drops on her knees "expecting Allen to thank God with her." He turns away, saying she may do the praying for both of them, then to her question "Don't you pray?" replies: "Oh, I don't talk about religion, you know." But he "had to tell her decisively before the week was out that he did not discuss religion. He had never thought of a wife as a person with whom one discussed things. He did not expect her to share his thoughts." Nor has he reckoned on listening to her thoughts. One morning she tells him of her pregnancy and looks forward to talking it all over with him each night. When he comes home late and sinks into a chair with a book, she reproaches him for lack of interest.

"My dear girl, that's a silly remark. I'm tired. And I know it's wonderful we are going to have a child, but really, I cannot talk about it all the time."
She gave him one outraged look. But it only irritated him further. He knew he had said something a bit off, but he could not help it. And if she went on like this all the time he would grow to hate the baby. He went on reading. She really must learn not to interrupt that. It was one of the things he could not stand.

The more she exasperates him, the more unreasonably he protects himself, until he is quite unpardonably keeping from her local news and family affairs, putting her at great disadvantage. But he does not alter her; he scarcely seems to try, withdrawal being the only self-defense he knows.

The novel's form is admirable. Allen and Marion are penned up together with their incompatibility for about twelve years in a district so unpeopled as to offer no ordinary diversion at all. Allen has his side exit into the gumdiggers' world; Marion has none. Every time he comes home he must face a wife whose values are anathema to him. If he tries too hard to attach Joan, his eldest and favorite child, he knows he endangers her: Joan, who has walked with him on the gumfield, takes to it alone for comfort, and is found alive only by chance—an episode which symbolically dramatizes the parents' tug-of-war over the child's personality. Allen is held here in the frontier's naked light, while his mind conducts its battles, right through the years which decide whether a man has made anything of his life.

Jane Mander hated suburbia, and seeing it settle in a country that had a chance to do without it, she set upon it as we do upon the first cases of an imported disease which we will later class as endemic. Marion as its symbol is excellently placed for the novel's purposes as she is misplaced for her own happiness. The author has rounded up in one woman the tendencies she saw in groups of local wives in the two previous novels.

Marion is from Auckland, but her parents had begun in real hardship in the backblocks; her mother, Mrs. Holt, who comes to stay, is full of rough, kind common sense, and is immediately held to be the better person. "I wonder why the pioneers never produce anything half so fine as themselves" is Geraldine's first reaction; Allen comes to the same viewpoint all too soon. Marion notices that her mother has made the more favorable impression on the firm's wives. "She did not understand it. Of course she loved her mother. But she was ashamed of her." That shame is the key; there are, then, absurd values in Marion, too deep, perhaps, to be teachable, though most of the time we are not sure of this. We see the surface errors, the genteel assumptions, but allied with so much loyalty and affection, and with such a desire to improve herself up to the level of Allen's sisters and his friends—all to please Allen who makes her feel inferior to them—that we cannot often see her as a hopeless case.

Geraldine Asbury and Nance Horton are good to her, of course, as pioneer neighbors; they meet her on arrival and have already been out to her house and stocked it with food. But when they visit her a few days later they leave cards, thinking she will feel slighted if they do not. This flusters Marion; she forces Allen to wire Auckland to have cards printed so that she may return their call properly. A Jane Austenlike problem in etiquette on the edge of a gumfield is simple realism—nothing got there faster—but if these women have the superior values we are asked to credit them with, why do they impose on Marion an example they will despise her for following?

It is often possible to come to a different conclusion from Jane Mander's on the given evidence about a character, though she is too honest a novelist to juggle the evidence or withhold what is vital. Marion's ordinariness, however, does seem to have cost her some of the compassion due to her from the author, as well as from her husband and his friends. She is set down, unprepared, in an isolation that is physically only a degree less than Alice Roland's, without a child of companionable age, nor any David Bruce or Mrs. Brayton. Geraldine and Nance are seven miles away in Pahi and think poorly of her anyway. There is no settlement around her at all—only a pub, a rough place for men to drink in, with its Mrs. Dubbins too harassed, too much of the immigrant servant to be her companion. Excluded from Allen's work, she is without the sense of partnership any farmer's wife would have. If he comes home, he reads. She has far less company than he and his friends who despise her discontent. She is as cut off from meaningful involvement as a suburban housewife, without any of the suburb's opportunities and panaceas.

Marion, in fact, seems as much the victim of snobbery as its purveyor. She is judged by the pioneer outlook which holds calm endurance of solitude to be a major virtue; applied to her also is a more subtle class snobbery that has always run through New Zealand life: that to need talk and company rather than books and one's own thoughts is the mark of an inferior background. Jane Mander was always concerned for the loneliness of cultured people in pioneer life; she seems unaware that the uncultured might suffer at least as much in these situations which were quite abnormal to the human race. There is, however, some melting toward Marion in the end:

He had worried a good deal about himself and Marion that winter. But that she was suffering as much in her way from starvation as he was in his did not occur to him, and that he was as inadequate to her development as she was to his had not dawned upon him. So that he could see no reason why she should be discontented with her life, or go seeking relief in other ways. She could have been taught, had it occurred to him that it was part of his business to teach his wife. He did not see that she, too, was making efforts to preserve some imagined ideal state in their relations. He was in danger of seeing in high relief only the things he disliked about her, her fanatical housekeeping, her curiosity, her carping criticism of Joan, her insidious criticism of their way of life. He could have done a good deal with her affectionateness and with her teachableness if he had only known how.

Auckland—which Allen had seen in his Oxford days as "conventional as any town in England"—stands in antithesis to their frontier home, and Marion's hankering for it damns her. Its trivial bustle obscures main issues, making it perhaps the better place for enduring what cannot be cured. In this spirit the author returns the Adairs to the city they came from, and soon it has "caught them all up in a flurry."

XII   *The Patron*

The beneficent gumfield patron and storekeeper, who is here the vehicle of the author's own dedication to the scene, is in his own right a figure she must have thought overdue for recognition. The power to exploit gumdiggers was such that legislation had been sought for their protection; commissions had shown that many bosses acted very creditably, but the unscrupulous could impress themselves more on the public mind. Upmore, the counterpart in Satchell's *The Land of the Lost*, is every kind of villain. In *The River* Jane Mander goes out of her way to say that "Roland had never exploited the squeezing possibilities of the arrangement made by the field owners and leasers for their own benefit. . . ." Her father and brother had shown her that power over men could be used with honor and generosity, and in *Allen Adair* she completes the testimony. Allen is another version of Jack Ridgefield of *The Passionate Puritan*, the trust-inspiring brother figure. But whereas Jack has specific technical skill in the dynamics of bush-felling which both supports his authority and makes him the instrument of change, Allen is static, nonspecialist, ministering most faithfully to the men who are least altering the landscape.

Allen Adair is inconsistent with the reputation Jane Mander had acquired in New Zealand for impropriety and feminism, and it might have softened the atmosphere if it had been her second novel. Its effective plea for a man's right to a modest vocation, un-

molested, comes from the same deep human concern as her pleas
for adventurous young women, reinforcing them. This was one
cause she could proclaim from outside the area of personal conflict,
drawing on the uncomplicated part of her love and loyalty, which
may account for this novel's singular harmony. Furthermore, it was
written while she was settling down in London, a city she found
"all to the good for the nerves." She wrote only about the kind of
people she knew best, and two of these types were being gratu-
itously misused by the New Zealand of her observation—the ardent,
brainy girls like herself, and the peaceable male misfits of the frontier. The same forces were hounding them both.

Jane Mander offered *Allen Adair* to New Zealand as an olive
branch and as an ultimatum. Here was a book that could shock
nobody, but if her country continued indifferent to books about
itself she would shift the scenery. It was too late for the guardians
of morals to trust her, and too soon—by at least thirty years—for
New Zealanders in general to want their own fiction. Her next
novel, therefore, was set in her second home, New York.

CHAPTER 4

Degrees of Marriage

Jane Mander wrote only of places she knew well; though loving change, quick with new people and situations and never outwardly confused, she could not move her characters about in a scene until she was physically and instinctively at home in it through domicile. Ten years in New York had given her the sure-footedness to build an imaginative structure upon her corner of it; moreover, her deep commitment to the city entitled her to express criticism as well as affection. It had been her home and a generous one, but she on her side had worked responsibly for its causes to the limits of her strength; in the balance sheet of stern conscience, rights taken must not exceed service given.

I *Conversations in Greenwich Village*

The group of young intellectuals who take the stage in *The Besieging City* are tossed around by the problems of their careers, by their love affairs, and almost equally by the state of the world, being of the type predisposed to suffer for the indignity of the international scene. In some places the themes are interwoven; in others the city wrestles with the cast for attention and often wins. The surface impression is of an immense ode to wartime and immediate postwar New York—strident, confused, exasperated, loving, admiring, and nostalgic.

The fictional self, Chris Mayne, is the leading character, responding to her surroundings with senses and intellect, though too often with nerves uppermost, being almost frantic with exhaustion. Her arguments against the city and against a tempting proposal of marriage take her logically to Europe at the end of the story. One of the coterie goes with her and two others go to Africa, all on the rational, talked-over level. "I know well that the city of New York will follow me and perhaps draw me back," says Chris, adding, of her friends, "all the people who can make money enough to live here will come back." But another verdict on New York—that it is a place of death—utters itself, perhaps involuntarily, if one sees as significant the number of fatalities in this story; and surely one should, as Jane Mander is little concerned with mortality elsewhere. Among the dozen or so central figures are two unrelated suicides, one street-accident death, and the loss of both mother and child in a first confinement; of the two children of a slightly older couple, one is an imbecile and the other has recently perished in a fire. No life renewal is ahead of the young group that fills the early chapters, and the gruesome, anonymous death of the elderly couple in the apartment next to Chris underlines a city's inhumanity to the old. As one reads the death roll it seems neither excessive nor planned; the episodes in themselves have little power to affect, but in retrospect they merge into a howl of protest against Megalopolis.

As a solution for the specialized type portrayed in Chris Mayne and some of her friends, whose deepest wish is to find their city endurable, Jane Mander gropes toward the evolution of a third sex. The journalist Redman Feltz, the most complicated and interesting study in the book, says: "Mentally at least we are breeding a bisexual creature, a composite, a third sex, and I believe we are doing it physically too . . . thank heaven, people like you and me can be left alone for five minutes without anyone assuming we would be found attempting to seduce each other. They may hurl the word decadent at us, my dear Christy, but I honestly think we are an advance on the breeders of sinners." She agrees: "I'm blessed if I can see what we are to keep the race going for . . . to shoot and gas itself off the earth in another twenty years' time." Redman goes on:

> Yes, and who is to decide which is ultimately better for the race . . . complexity or simplicity, maleness or femaleness, or a composite? If humanity is to go on, a lot of the masculine element will have to go. It is necessary in a pioneer and fighting age. But we are beginning to repudiate the warlike section. America repudiates it absolutely. If we are to have beauty and peace we must cultivate the artists and the feminine element in the race.

Redman and Chris live by this ideal of noncommitment to the conventionally defined male and female roles; others in the group, unfixed in their path, less analytical, avoid standard solutions, requiring their friendships to support unusual intensity. All the material components of *The Besieging City* are the antithesis of *Allen*

Adair's, but both novels are aspects of one persuasion: that there is room in the world for the atypical to evolve a peaceful destiny, unmolested.

In place of development and a sense of time passing, there is here a set piece in which a group forms and then disperses, broken up by personal disasters inconsequentially, it would seem, unless one accepts the city's malevolence. While they are in motion they are deftly handled; the crowded scene with its argumentative vitality is a new aspect of Jane Mander—not one she could have turned appropriately to the New Zealand she knew where vitality was still very physical in form, and eccentricities the fruit of solitariness. She believed this to be her best book technically; one could agree. Yet a number of characters quickly sketched and attended to do not in this case compensate for the want of one deeply explored and followed through. The material is in these people; almost any of them is worth a much closer knowledge. Chris Mayne's obstructive egotism, very like Valerie Carr's, is part of the barrier to one's better acquaintance with them, and the scheme of the book forms the rest, for one must allow that New York itself has a dominant role. In managing the ambitious theme the author has been tempted into a self-conscious virtuosity which has not the simple propulsion to take the book very far from its own times. For all its skill and sincerity of purpose, it is likely to remain overlooked in the crowded company of lesser novels about New York.

II A South Kensington Coterie

There is little striving for effect in *Pins and Pinnacles*, a story about the personal lives of some London intellectuals for the devourers of easy reading. The author made no bones about it: "I cannot claim to have written the story with any profundity," she wrote to a New Zealand paper on its publication. "It is done from the outside and is not burdened with a lot of analyses and introspection. It is a story of human relation and has a good deal of suspense leading up to a crisis. It is, I suppose, quite healthy in tone and I doubt if it will shock even New Zealanders. I regard it as certainly the most saleable book I have written."[1] By 1938 she was dubbing it something done "just to end an unsatisfactory publisher's contract."[2] She obviously wanted to stay in the running as a novelist, and if this book bought her a year or two's respite from hack work she could write a better one. But it had only moderate success with the public aimed at and not much validity for any other.

The scene is an expensive little cul-de-sac in South Kensington inhabited by Mirabel Heath; her publisher Paul Daley; and John Craik, Paul's closest friend, whom he is trying to rescue from insanity. A promising cast is assembled in well-chosen positions, but nothing is developed in depth. Mirabel Heath is one of the hundreds of heroines of the 1920's whose allure a modern reader can believe in only by an act of faith. John Craik's neurasthenia, a promising study to begin with, becomes merely a part of plot machinery. The Mander talent lights up only in Julius Vaughan, the beautiful young writer who accepts as his due all that his older and influential friends do for him, only to crumple whenever he suspects them of not thinking him perfect. The author was too tired now and too remote from her sources of power for more than the odd flicker. Yet the novel has the specious technical superiority that can come from not aiming too high and the virtue, here sadly negative, of taking the background for granted because nobody needs London to be explained.

III   *The Fictional Self*

Mirabel Heath nevertheless adds a few strokes to the composite portrait of the fictional self—the fair, blue-eyed, outspoken long-distance walker who is at the center of five novels. The resemblance to Jane Mander is the most complete in the child Asia who contains the potentialities of all the others before any determining choice has been made; Asia the young woman, Sidney Carey, Valerie Carr, Chris Mayne, and Mirabel are the imaginative outcome of separate trends of the author's personality. The technique is more patent than in most writers, perhaps because there was so much else unfixed in the material that the stabilizing quasi-autobiographical viewpoint had to be clung to. It also forestalls certain kinds of presumptuousness; Mirabel of London is part American, Chris of New York is some sort of English nomad who has lived in Australia, thus disclaiming any interpretative authority beyond what they have won by domicile and affection, which is as far as the author would take it herself. In all cases the heroine's milieu is within her experience and her occupation very close to, if not identical with, one the author had tried.

The young women's diversities of job and location are only the necessary paraphernalia; the agitating theme is marriage, each variation of the self exploring some alternative to New Zealand-style marriage, which was rigid enough to account for any extravagances in the revolt. Money and servants make no difference—which is part of what *The Strange Attraction* says—if society is bent on controlling the ensuing leisure. Where society is the enemy the proposing man cannot offer protection to the woman who surrenders her independence for him; his proposal can be enough in itself to put him among the enemy in her mind. This happens to Dane Barrington intermittently, and once and for all to Gerald Lloyd whom Chris Mayne rejects with hysterical discourtesy after being very happy living with him. The revulsion here is beyond what anything in the New York scene appears to account for, except that Gerald has hinted at a home in California where he finds his best commissions as an architect; Chris may be carrying associations from another country. But she makes it plain that it is marriage, not Gerald, she is against; her love will go into friendships and into writing.

Is it significant that the two who marry into England go meekly to the altar? Mirabel Heath is the most mellow of the heroines; her marriage to Paul will not harm her career, and she will continue as a well-to-do London sophisticate with a profession. Thus the readers of *Pins and Pinnacles* have their conventional happy ending without loss of principle in the author. Sidney Carey, the least unusual of the heroines, likewise accepts a marriage which offers her comfortable status in England besides the sense of mission she requires.

Asia and Allen enter a partnership which may never lead to children nor even to setting up house together. It cannot be said that she has sought this anomalous position, but the wretchedness of her mother's unloving marriage predisposes her to see hope in its opposite. A key to these situations is that the fictional self is unmoved by the normal desire for children; hence she can choose her ground. Chris Mayne's choice is unequivocal; Asia's real decision may be years ahead; but Valerie, the only one whose marriage is seen in progress, is being put to the test on this.

Valerie's marriage with Dane falls apart, we feel, not because love burns itself out (which is her fear) but because it cannot make a woman of her. Dane needs mothering; his upbringing by an itinerant, absent-minded father puts an element of the orphan boy into his notorious appeal for women. It is clear that she cannot save him from himself unless she can be in some ways the older woman.

The temptation is insidious, but a career girl might be less set back by two or three children than by making a child of a husband. We see Dane trying to protect her from his needs; this marriage is his final bid to become as mature emotionally as he is intellectually, by asking nothing of Valerie that it at all inconveniences her to give. From the beginning she is absolved from having children; Dane's ménage absolves her from all domesticity. All she has to contend with is herself: if she gives him what he is too proud to ask for, she is bound to him by delight in giving. The affair reads strangely, as if they can turn their passions on and off at will, which is perhaps the truth of it if she will not be tempted out of girlhood to meet his deeper need.

IV   *Is This Feminism?*

Though the voice of the modern young woman rings through the novels, the feminist pleas are limited to the cause of these few exceptional people who ask to be excused conformity. The emphasis is different from that of other early New Zealand novelists such as Edith Searle Grossman and Jean Devanny, who are concerned with the state of women in conventional marriage. The only two conventionally married women Jane Mander considers are Alice Roland and Marion Adair. The former's unhappiness is due to an unsuitable husband; we can imagine her living very contentedly even in Pukekaroro's rough isolation, given a congenial partner. Marion Adair is even more strongly wife and mother; Allen treats her quite badly, which the author admits with her sense of justice but not with her sympathies, because Marion is not the type of woman she will take up arms for.

The novels do not concern themselves with women's rights in general. New Zealand women had those rights, and Jane Mander was boasting about them from soapboxes around New York before the books were written. When she sat down as a novelist she had to consider whether society had progressed to that acceptance of the atypical which makes the rights worth having, and the answer to this was unhopeful. In 1924 William Pember Reeves summed matters up:

On the whole the most marked feature of their use of the franchise is their tendency to agree with their menkind. . . . Families, as a rule, vote together, and the women of any class or section are swayed by its interests,

prejudices, or ideals to just about the same extent as the males thereof. . . .
They do less platform-speaking than Englishwomen do, though many of
them study public affairs—about which, to say truth, they have much to
learn. Observers outside the Dominion need not suppose that New Zealand
women are in the least degree either "wild" or "new" or belong to any
shrieking sisterhood. Though one or two have entered learned professions,
most of them are engaged in domestic duties. Those who go out into the
world do so to work unassumingly as school teachers, factory hands, or
household servants.[3]

This gives the very flavor of the pattern maintained almost uni-
formly in the New Zealand Jane Mander left, stayed away from, and
returned to in the 1930's to ask in anguish whether its women were
to go down in history as a race of cake-makers. The answer to that
has been yes, on the whole. In the present decade women are still
pressed into the very domestic, homogeneous mold of the frontier:
practical virtues prevail; no quarter is given and none is asked. Overseas visitors from reputedly backward societies drop in to marvel at
New Zealand social gatherings, where men and women withdraw to
opposite sides of the room and spend the evening in entirely separate conversations. This convention, at its most severe in country
areas, dominant in mercantile and university circles, has broken
down only in the arts—a community of fairly recent growth. The
pattern for women is still so tight that mental hospital superinten-
dents recently have protested at the preponderance of women pa-
tients, and in 1968 one publicly referred to them as "the Negroes of
New Zealand society."[4]

If to the cake-makers New Zealand women have added one other
group of specialists—novelists—the reason may be the very harsh-
ness by which the pattern is defined. The social consequences of
minor deviations are so great that a woman might as well go as far
as she wants and write as she pleases; it will cost her no more. But
having accepted quasiexcommunication she may have less at stake
than a man, not having a family to support partly on the earnings
from conventional sources, to which extremity New Zealand may
owe the fact that its women novelists are held to be the more adventurous. The local problem is one that will not yield to treatment by
feminism because the rigidity is applied and maintained largely by
women themselves. There is enough of Alice Roland in most New
Zealand women to make them very susceptible to pressures to do
everything the hard way and to see that everyone else does: the

mother-punishment doctrines which for a while dominated the Plunket Society (and defeated there, made their home in the Play Centre Association) are administered mainly by women; it is in women's organizations and in those aspects of suburban life which women have entirely in their own hands that the deviator, or the specialist in any skills outside the pattern, is given the least acceptance. This is what makes Jane Mander's books still profoundly true and relevant, assailing as they do both the "disease of Puritanism" and conformity for its own sake.

Feminist is a troublesome word: one cannot know precisely what another's mind holds as the womanly norm which will determine its application. To the extent that Jane Mander believed in the opportunity to vote and to be educated she was perhaps a feminist in her day, though for a long time now the state has seen these rights as obligations. All she asks outside that is that society, or the family as its representative, should not impose a uniform contract on the odd misfit—that if a woman would rather have a profession than husband and children it is better for everyone that she follow her vocation—a humble enough plea. But her removal to countries where individuality was better provided for in no way mitigated the urgency of her spirit, because as an expatriate she could only work for the day when her own country would be varied and flexible enough to contain her.

CHAPTER 5

Influence and Opinion

I N the survey this chapter attempts of the influences Jane Mander was involuntarily exposed to, those she consciously sought, and her later conclusions about them, her supporting evidence is scrappy though often pungent. Her failure to write reminiscences,[1] combined with a lifelong aversion to the indulgence of introspection, leaves us without a central personal testament. A deep respect for privacy—one of the most lasting influences of her up-bringing— together with abundant loyalty and kindness, co-existed with a Shavian determination to put the world right by outspokenness, even by shock if necessary. Yet just as in conversation her exuberant loquacity stopped short of confidences—at least of the kind that would interest us now—so in her nonfictional writings she hurled herself into what was going on currently around her.

The functional brevity of her letters strengthens the supposition that even if people had persuaded her toward an analytically retrospective view of her life (which scarcely anyone in her later years was interested enough to do) the result would have been unfruitful. Her most outgoing comments about her early days occur in light-hearted interviews she gave to papers when her books were being published, when she was still cheerful about her prospects as a novelist and overseas readers were interested in her outlandish childhood. After her return to New Zealand there was no encouragement for anything of this kind; only a good cause had the power to tempt her now—hence the invaluable series of articles in the Christchurch *Press* of 1934,[2] impelled by the sorry state of New Zealand society and literature. In such a case, with all her energies turned outward, she would toss off the odd personal comment, no less illuminating for being a by-product. Similarly in the mass of her routine reviews, an occasional remark would pertinently erupt, showing how thin the crust still was over the molten issues her best fiction sprang from.

The novels properly remain her major testament, their virtues and defects truly reflecting the society that shaped her. Other observers of that society, including more recent analysts quoted below, can confirm what she knew at first hand—the more so as her isolated northern communities turned out to be by no means atypical of the nation in many of their trends. Like any other writer struggling out of the frontier to a position from which she could portray it in perspective, she needed a helping hand from other cultures. As a New Zealander she was reared on English books. Australia helped her discover herself, and in New York she got down seriously to writing, in between singular encounters with moments of history on Morningside Heights, in Greenwich Village, and up-state.

I *A Slow Beginning*

In her austere and virtuously busy childhood there was little scope for idle writing, and Jane Mander was hampered all her life by the want of ordinary facility which early practice might have given her. Certainly her school essays had been read aloud to the class—her first triumph in a nonutilitarian field and one she remembered later when she clutched at writing as a way out of her colonial dilemma. Her first attempt at storytelling was a nightly serial, told to her brother in bed through the flimsy partition of one of the converted sheds they lived in—a romantic tale of foreign lands and tigers. In her late teens she won a newspaper's Christmas story competition, then let fiction lapse until in the tower of the Whangarei house, at nearly thirty, she began the novel she later submitted in London and scrapped in New York. Everyday journalism occupied several of the intervening years, and not one item of this is traceable: the *Northern Advocate*'s files for the four relevant years were destroyed, as were the files of the *North Auckland Times* that contained her Dargaville journalism.

The earliest writing of Jane Mander's so far traced is a letter written to the *Triad* when she was thirty-two. It is where one would expect to find her; this monthly romped pointedly among the arts in New Zealand for a few years, taunting the derivative dullness of other local journalism, until it transferred to Sydney, leaving a gap unfilled for decades. Reviewing *The Strange Attraction* from Sydney in 1923, the *Triad* recalled that "A few years ago Miss Mander was a young girl stuck away in one of those queer old places north of

Auckland, and we used to write to her about her promise, and she used to write to us about our soul. . . ."[3] The *Triad* had an eye for promise: it had already published some embryonic Katherine Mansfield. The issue of December 1, 1909 carried this *cri de coeur* from the north:

A Lost October

Dear TRIAD: I'm sorry you live in Dunedin, because if you were anywhere handy there are things I might mention. You have not deprived me critically of my "presence" or my "temperament" or my "soul." Don't keep such things in stock to be flattened gold leaf like, under your Thorry touch. My only accomplishment is the joy of life and that you have sadly marred. Where is my October TRIAD? Where is my Art Supplement? What have I ever done to the TRIAD but seize it from the post, and, deserting all else, rejoice in it alone? Why, the only thing that keeps me from preaching temperance, or making draughty garments for the superfluous heathen, or marrying a Sunday School teacher in this brain-benumbing, stimulus-stifling, sense-stultifying, soul-searing silence is the invasion of the TRIAD and its kind. Be good to me and send it along on the wings of a Wellington wind. And, please, publish some more short poems by Oscar Wilde. And please take great care of Frank Morton. There's a man I could live with and love, especially if he did the cooking. I live in hopes of "dining out" with him some day. Then life in New Zealand would have produced *the* compensation. Don't die yet, either of you. That TRIAD please.
Yours in the things worth while,
J. Mander.

Whangarei.

She escaped again to Sydney at about this time and, under the name "Manda Lloyd," wrote for the *Maoriland Worker*,[4] a Wellington Labour weekly, where the youthful Bob Semple and M. J. Savage rubbed shoulders with apposite extracts from Olive Schreiner and Bernard Shaw. In one long article in 1911 she describes a day spent in the children's court in Sydney where a series of underfed boys are charged with such offenses as riding a tram without paying, using bad language, and setting off fire-crackers in the street. The magistrate examines and judges them on their knowledge of the Ten Commandments and the multiplication table. Although propaganda keeps on breaking through—"There will always be thousands of unwanted children under the capitalist system"—parts of the article suggest that Jane Mander already realized how effective a fictional arrangement of a human episode could be. Then in the case of three youngsters charged with stealing vegetables she simply strides out after humbug:

In summing up to all three the fossil emphasised the enormity of a breach of the Sabbath (this in a city notorious for its unorthodox behaviour on Sundays), and the shamefulness of worrying the poor Chinamen (this, ye gods! in a country that's doing its best to worry every Chinaman out of it, that insults foreigners every week in its public press, where not one person in a thousand speaks of an alien as a fellow creature, and where the whole atmosphere reeks of contempt for the "poor Chinaman!")[5]

In the same journal on July 21, 1911, she tells of her conversion to socialism three years before in Sydney where she heard it preached for the first time. This article, "A Woman's View," is innocently illuminating of her state of mind prior to this encounter, revealing as it does a temperament unlikely to align itself for long to any political movement or system: "I knew nothing of Socialism. I was entirely in sympathy with all people who worked, for I had worked myself, had been poor enough to go to bed in the dark to save candles, had owned but one pair of shoes at a time. My environment improved considerably, but I realised that I was still up against forces that hampered my individuality; that things were all wrong somehow. . . ."[6]

She was now preparing to go to America. Socialism helped her define her quest and find a niche as a writer—these were unpaid articles, impelled by belief. She was to detach herself from the movement as such, perhaps inevitably, to assume the nonaffiliated stand of the novelist. But it would be a mistake to see her affair with socialism as a mild matter and unduly late in life. Though New Zealand as an entity was fairly enough regarded as Socialist by the rest of the world, this group she was now in touch with was looked on within New Zealand as ominously revolutionary and godless. She had moved some distance from her origins.

II *Religion*

The Mander children went regularly to whatever Protestant church was available; the allegiance to the Congregational Church that Frank and Janet Mander started out with could not survive unbroken as they moved through isolated communities where various sects took their turn in the school room or local hall. Kaiwaka in 1878 built a little interdenominational church on the road to Hakaru where the congregation sat under such itinerant ministers as could reach them, with laymen to fill in. Then in Port Albert the Manders were in the bosom of the Albertland Settlement whose ideal was the unsectarian church: "The same congregation that one Sunday sat under the Rev. William Worker of the Wesleyan connection and the following week maybe under that Anglican stalwart, Chas. Haseldon, the village schoolteacher, would on another Sunday listen with pleasure and profit to Presbyterian doctrine expounded by the local sawmiller, John Hunter Penman, and finish the month with one of Spurgeon's sermons, feelingly rendered by the young Quaker, W. B. Farrand."[7] Frank Mander took his turn at conducting services and preaching. Later he developed facility for writing religious verses which he printed to give to friends; these suggest the very personal approach to the Bible of a man unused to leaning on a church or its ministers for exposition.[8] A relative pressed to define Frank Mander's religion replied that "Really he needed a church all to himself."

Jane's nomadic course through churches reluctant to fix procedures and doctrine left her lightly bound by formal religion. She had not even a fixed parish's old supporting families to reckon with as a girl growing up in town might have had; she could make an unrancorous exit from organized religion and pursue the enemy outside the church walls. The article of 1916, "A Diary of Evolution," which can surely be credited with some biographical significance, shows various beliefs evolving through stages of discovery without any sharp encounter with specific doctrinal pressure.[9]

To understand the nature of the pressure we should study the case of Sidney Carey versus the church as amiably put in *The Passionate Puritan*. Sidney, who has broken with her church in Auckland, keeps clear of Puhipuhi's Sunday services which are held in her school room; she can apparently abstain without ruffling the village. But then comes a Sunday when a visiting curate is due.

Word had gone round that the curate was a good speaker and that Arthur Devereux would sing. . . . More than a hundred men from the bush and the mill were gathered there, and most of the village, for the Nonconformist section had no prejudices about hearing any brand of doctrine. They were only too glad of a diversion. There was not half enough room for the congregation. . . . She felt, as she sat at her window watching, that she was missing something, that she could have let her consistency lapse for once.

People talk about this service for a long time afterward and she is "always absurdly annoyed that she had missed it." The Ridgefields had not asked her to dinner with Arthur afterward. "She knew that they had very little room, and she knew she had made scornful remarks in their hearing about churches and clergy in general. But still she was chagrined to be left out. . . . It amused her to discover that she hated to be left out of something." Arthur brings the curate to see her in the afternoon, they joke unstuffily about her absence, and Sidney finds the curate as knowledgeable as herself about current Australian art and writing.

Sidney will assuredly capitulate to this sociable, undemanding churchgoing; but she must slink off to a hidden gully if she wants to smoke, and the socially adept Mana sends her children quickly out of the room when she sees Sidney about to accept a cigarette from Arthur. " 'The deuce! I forgot they went to school,' said Arthur, after they had gone out. 'They might talk,' said Mana. 'They wouldn't mean—' " This comes much nearer the real issue.

III   "A Thing in Itself"

In "Fiction and the Social Pattern" (*Landfall*, March, 1953), Robert Chapman admirably sets out the origins and prevailing codes of the main immigrant surge of the 1860's and 1870's, the very people who made Jane Mander's northern milieu. He demonstrates how "In the face of the industrial revolution the doctrine of work was elaborated and the sins of the flesh extended to encompass all the pleasures which might divert the energies from the arid struggle to survive. . . . Sex and drink and ease-taking led to terrestrial and eternal damnation both. In the overcrowded squalid conditions where much moral backsliding was accompanied by much grinding failure there was a high rate of emotional acceptance of the proposition which connected immorality and failure as cause and effect. . . ." Professor Chapman goes on to point out that this moral scheme survived the emigrant journey better than the churches themselves with their appurtenances, that the churches in fact "tended increasingly over the decades to be left out" until they were "no longer in sufficiently vital contact with enough New Zealanders to alter the design of the pattern. Somewhere about the turn of the century or possibly later (though the failure of the Church-sponsored attempt to introduce nation-wide Prohibition seems to indicate the first decade at the latest) the pattern can be considered

a thing in itself. It was by then unconsciously assumed and beyond
the redirection of changing Churches which might have supervised
and readjusted it in happier circumstances." Pioneer circumstances
had given puritan morality an "obvious sanction. In the new land
and with the new tasks it fitted, it worked. 'Work, deny yourself
and you will be prosperous and saved' presided as a motto over the
cracking of the spine of the bush."

Immigrants in sufficient numbers to set the prevailing tone came
out of one country at one point in its history, at the very moment
when the main part of the north was inviting settlers. Dr. Samuel
Edger wrote in honest conviction of his Albertlanders: "Do not
think that there is unanimity of religion—quite the opposite. We
have all shades of opinion, but our diversities are not dissen-
sions."[10] But in fact the diversities were only those possible among
mid-nineteenth-century British Protestants. Non-Christians—that is
to say foreigners with some other positive religious belief—were
never encountered. Even foreign Christians were too rare to be an
influence. The only considerable body of foreigners in the north
were a few thousand "Austrians" (as they then unwillingly were,
ancestors of the present Dalmatians) who took to the gumfields,
upsetting tradition by digging diligently in groups and saving their
earnings to bring out relatives; language, apart from anything else,
kept them to themselves.

The settlers' homogeneity, combined with the austerities imposed
by circumstances, precluded influences which might have counter-
acted any patent manifestations of puritanism brought in, and there
were such in Jane Mander's family. The Kerrs brought with them a
picture forty-one inches by twenty-eight called *The Last Judgment*.
This is a vast double view of heaven and earth; in the background is
heaven, pale and tranquil, and in the foreground a ravine-split view
of tormented earth. At the top of the landscape Christ is throned,
flanked by angels and pews full of stiff crowned figures. In the cloud
under him a huge, revengeful figure in black Geneva gown and
bands holds a thunderbolt. In the foreground are the decorous
saved, some of them wearing the white ruffs and black cloaks of
seventeenth-century Puritans. On the ravine's jagged rocks below
climb or fall the damned. These include half-draped ladies falling
in fear, sumptuously dressed clerics with their gold crosses showing,
and at least one pope outflung amongst a jumble of golden vessels
and money scattered from the hands of the fallen figures.[11]

The picture was over the mantelpiece at Ramarama when the Maori raiders came through; footmarks showed that they had assembled to gaze, and it was the only object they left intact. It was there for Jane to gaze at as a child, and it was in grandfather Kerr's house in Newton when she stayed there as a young woman. In this latter period she took her sister Anne to a concert of the Clay Bell-ringers in Saint Benedict's Hall, and her grandfather prayed loudly each day for a week for their souls because they had been inside property owned by the Church of Rome.

But the anticleric—as well as the specifically anti-Catholic—feeling around her now was out of its historical context, inapposite. One can imagine her suffering martyrdom as an early Puritan, but to a girl looking for a positive belief there was nothing in this modern secularized puritanism for its own sake. The vivid picture of hell can be said to have persisted in her as a basis for repudiation; each of her novels proclaims that there is no hell but what people make for themselves and each other. Away from their traditional opponents, safe in religious supremacy, the settlers might have disarmed themselves and encouraged a new flowering of the purely religious spirit. In a way it did flower, though outside the churches now, by imbuing the laws of the country with much practical Christianity, but the people kept themselves armed out of habit in case any "live and let live" cropped out in the community.

In some notes on religion in New Zealand writing, Dennis McEldowney in 1966 placed Jane Mander neatly:

The first real writer to demonstrate that what no longer moves will soon be moved against was Jane Mander. Her young women witness in Northland bush communities to the concept of God as Force with about the same de-gree of intensity as they witness to their liberation by smoking cigarettes; her real attack was on the "disease" of puritanism, which to her destroyed spontaneity in behaviour. Her language on this theme is remarkably mod-ern, which is one of the reasons—although the main reason is that she was a genuine novelist—why *The Story of a New Zealand River* remains readable. With her, as with Jessie Mackay but in reverse, the social implications of religion were more important than the primary belief.[12]

"God as Force" is a vague doctrine and counters a doctrine too amorphous to lay hold of in terms of religious argument; but the cigarette or the glass of ale will bring the adversary into the open at once, so that is where the fight is. Where a novel relies too much on these skirmishings, as *The Strange Attraction* does at times, the heroine risks looking silly and as negative as what she opposes. A great strength of *The River* is the all-around buildup of the adversary so that one sees Asia as positive; *The Passionate Puritan*, though lighter in every way, achieves a comparable balance.

The novels seek primarily to capture and hold one position ahead of the status quo; they advocate the right to believe in happiness and to seek it according to one's nature which would be quite simple if other people would forget about retribution and do the same. As Asia says: "Mother has taught me one great lesson. I'm done with misery. I shall have nothing more to do with it as long as I live. I shall train my mind to ignore it. I won't cease to help people, or to be sympathetic, but I'm not going to suffer over anybody any more."

IV *Quid pro Quo*

The freedom granted these independent characters has one severe condition; they must pull their weight. The accounts are kept strictly and must balance. Asia earns her freedom, if ever a girl did, by loyalty and capability through the household's lean years. It is always emphasized that she does her chores before asking for anything. When she goes off to join her lover for a few days, she first spends the morning cooking enough food to keep the family going for some time; on her first break from home she accounts for herself to Mrs. Brayton:

. . . I *have* waited, and I *have* suppressed myself. I'm not rushing off at the first impulse. I've done everything I could to please her, been a beastly hypocrite and lied—ugh! And I've managed her husband for her. And I'm not leaving her alone or in a hole of any kind. Things are better at home than they have ever been—the girls are growing up and Elsie is three and no more sign of babies. I've thought it all out, and I've waited. You don't think I'm a brute, do you?

The principals of the other novels are excused this direct service to their families. Sidney Carey, Mirabel Heath, and Chris Mayne are already orphaned; Valerie Carr has wealthy parents whose demands are different; but all have their account with society which we see them paying in common currency. They keep out of debt and require nobody to tidy up after them; they are conspicuously good at the routine side of their occupations. Asia has every kind of domestic skill and a profession; Sidney is the most highly graded teacher of her year; Valerie runs a paper well and does something brilliant with the job-printing contracts; Chris Mayne is an executive in the Red Cross and a reliable journalist. Each has the kind of ability that must rate them high in a simple society's judgment. Only on these premises are we asked to grant that they are exceptional characters in other respects, entitled to individual thought and action in what time and opportunity is left.

Nowhere are we asked to admire the mere dreamer or esthete, nor the specialized person who is vague by ordinary standards but in some one art supremely right. Nowhere is it allowed that charm is a legitimate weapon, nor that many people like to be won that way; her leading women are credited with charm but they drop it to prevail by argument and equity. Jane Mander herself was supremely happy in the world of the arts, among people whose behavior was outwardly unpredictable and whose debt to society could be paid in their individual currency only. She could not use them in her novels because she could not speak in them. Necessity and precept had fixed in her young the habit of pulling her weight in practical ways. "Our life did not encourage the specialist," she wrote. "The genius was the person who could build houses, pull out teeth, mend boots, cook a meal, and bind up broken limbs. Self-reliance was developed as a matter of course. The list of my accomplishments as a child of ten would look so incredible now that I will leave it out."[13]

A few New Zealanders of her generation opted out of the local contract, deciding early that they were special cases, put up with being labeled dreamy or unsatisfactory, and proved themselves right much later, as Katherine Mansfield did, or proved nothing but that New Zealand had no place for them. It was perhaps inevitable that Jane Mander should go about it the other way, more than proving herself by local standards before she became a writer. There is a strong parallel here with *The River* where Asia's emergence as a professional pianist takes one by surprise, so busy has she been proving herself in other ways.

The battle within herself was never won. Conscience jolted Jane Mander whenever anything soft came her way. Nobody could have worked harder to round out abilities, but the complementary education was almost always at odds with circumstances and instincts. Her writing remained primarily the product of early abilities: self-reliance, humanitarian concern, and vigorous thinking.

V   *The Bookshelf*

The everyday book of Jane's childhood was the Bible, used quietly by her mother, evangelically by her father, and by herself for extensive memorizing. The only other books she knew before she was ten were the boxful that went with the family by punt or cart to be put on the sitting-room mantelpiece—when they had a sitting room. These were: Shakespeare; *The Pilgrim's Progress*; and Cruden's Concordance, *Peep of Day* and *Line upon Line*; Collier's history of England and a life of Alexander the Great; *Villette*, *Wuthering Heights*, and *Vanity Fair*; Tennyson, Longfellow, Cowper, Elizabeth Barrett Browning, and Mrs. Hemans; and a verse anthology from which her father used to recite. *On the Banks of the Amazon* and two old copies of *The Boy's Own Paper* came her way next; she looked with nostalgia from London to the days when a book was a "magnificent event."[14]

Until she left Pukekaroro she was restricted to what the family owned, being too young to be fed from Mrs. Clayton's library as Asia was from Mrs. Brayton's; and indeed though Mrs. Brayton is a faithful portrait of Mrs. Clayton as to appurtenances and general style, there is enough about her, besides her promotion of Voltaire, to suggest that she was touched up by memory of that old rip Miss Crawley from *Vanity Fair* on the mantelpiece. In Port Albert and Mangere more books were about; the younger sisters remember them always being plentiful. Any such neighborhood could muster up the major English novels of the century, plenty of factual literature and poetry, besides a good range of boys' adventure stories which the girls always read. By her late teens Jane Mander had access to the resources of Auckland itself, approximate to those of an English provincial city.

All her writings about books reinforce the impression of her novels: that though she was receptive to new forms in fiction and in the theater, she was more excited by novelty of content, whether it was the sight of human beings in a new social or geographical situation, or an old situation excavated in depth by modern psychological equipment. As her own ambition was to apply a modern intellect to a very new (though still quite old-fashioned) society in a previously unrecorded environment, she had enough complexity without trying for a new form.

Her admiration for Olive Schreiner's novel (which she may not have read young) seems to have become fuel in the immense drive to get her own written. There is no sign that her work is directly influenced by *The Story of an African Farm*, nor even by Lyndall, and it is scarcely to be expected. We may see Olive Schreiner's tragic inconclusiveness as nearer the human condition than most of the novels that came out of Western society's optimism; but Jane Mander's fiercely sanguine temperament exploring a very hopeful society could see tragedy as accidental and a satisfactory outcome plausible in most situations.

She had little patience with the minor literature of new countries if it missed stature by playing up external features and by dodging the human ones, or if in establishing national types it became obscure to readers of goodwill outside. A novel had to be built to keep afloat in the main stream, and one must study the structure of the ones that managed. In the early 1920's she became exasperated with the Australians, considering them obdurately local, but as Henry Handel Richardson built up her great Australian saga she greeted it with delight and homage. Reaffirmed praises of Henry Handel Richardson indicate an attitude to the making of national literature: local materials, international method.[15]

VI   Trans-Tasman and Trans-Pacific

The influence of her time in Sydney speaks for itself in quite obvious ways in the first three novels. Even in *The Besieging City* Chris Mayne is given a vaguely Australian background to account for a viewpoint of New York which is not wholly British nor quite of New Zealand either. Dane Barrington of *The Strange Attraction* comes in with an Australian-made reputation, bolstered by tastes and attitudes which look incongruous in North Auckland, as they are meant to.

Asia Roland has already had two years in Australia when Allen Ross and Barrie Lynne turn up at Pukekaroro. At the first sight of her they are impressed and wonder how she can have such style if she is a local girl. On meeting them Asia tells Allen that she has seen him often before, in Sydney. " 'Ah.' And both men felt that much was explained." Later Asia and Allen plan their joint future: "They talked of the awakening of humanity through the teachings of socialism, of the hopelessness of established systems, of the great future before the Labour Party of New South Wales. And that brought them to themselves and the part that Ross, and through him she, too, would play in it." Arthur Devereux, the Englishman of *The Passionate Puritan*, brings a visiting curate to call on Sidney Carey. Arthur has not been to her cottage before and he is impressed with her books, which include some he knew nothing of. "The curate picked up that book of remarkable drawings by the Australian artist, Norman Lindsay. . . . In his wanderings Arthur had somehow managed to miss the peculiar genius of Australia. He had heard of the Sydney Bulletin, of course, but thought it rotten taste, and left it there. He had heard of Lindsay Gordon, of Rolfe Boldrewood, and Henry Lawson. But of the clever modern school of Australian cartoonists, etchers, painters, and sculptors he knew next to nothing, and he sat back and listened humbly. . . ." The curate knows the password; it makes a basis for an afternoon's flirtation which Arthur has to watch and "his attitude of mind towards her underwent a somersault that afternoon."

These episodes make their point, that Australia is a handy place for a bright young New Zealander's awakening, and though the majority might deplore the trans-Tasman scene, there was an active minority interested in it: the editors of the *Triad*, for instance, and many journalists who reverenced the high-styled cockiness of the Sydney *Bulletin*, aiming their best writing at it. Jane Mander had done this without luck, and in 1923, reviewing creative writing in Australia and New Zealand, she wrote: "For fifty years that unique weekly paper has nursed the leading verse and story writers of the country. . . . As it was for years the only possible market for original stuff, men had to write for it or go unheard." But by now she thought that "it kept its own sons too much to the aboriginal."

It demanded the oaths of goldfield, the raw meat of the squatters' camps, the crude tragedy of Larrikin love. Blasphemous and disrespectful it has been and remains to all that savors of imitation and soppiness and make-believe. . . . It gave men a fine training in condensation. But it took, and led them to produce, stuff that could be published nowhere else. For it is largely written in Australian slang, as unintelligible to readers in other countries as the Yorkshire Weekly, or Gaelic, or J. A. V. Weaver.[16]

In the same article she sees Australian literature as having become static, "almost entirely narrative and descriptive," its writers untouched by the "New Psychology." "We have numberless unwritten novels in the eternal struggle of the refined and cultured

English with the pioneer environment. But no Australian writer
has yet got behind the man in that struggle. The newcomer who
can not light a fire is simply a subject for gibes."[17]

It seems, then, that the stimulus Australia supplied was to Jane
Mander's personal development, by encouraging her to find her
own path and follow it, for which she could remain grateful while
repudiating its general literary trends. Her debt to the United States
of America was more complex; here again direct literary influence
is unacknowledged and hard to discern. In 1934, in reply to an article of A. R. D. Fairburn's, she went so far as to say that she was
"alarmed at the idea of advising writers to study American models
unless they stick to the books of that lovely writer of English, Willa
Cather."[18] Her own novels were on the whole cut to a basic pattern,
a composite of the less-than-great English novels, to which she tried
to accommodate her material. Katherine Mansfield justly complained that "she leans too hard on England. There are moments
when we catch a bewilderingly vivid glimpse of what she really felt
and knew . . . but we suspect these are moments when she is off her
guard. Then her real talent flashes out; her characters move
quickly, almost violently. . . ."[19]

No other critic has so aptly isolated *The River*'s explosive content
from its obligation to describe conventionally. It is tenable that the
off-guard moments were born of Jane Mander's attachment to the
Washington Square Players and the Provincetown Players while
she was writing this novel. A young woman denied theater, brought
up even to suspect it, is suddenly exposed to one of its most dynamic
phases, to theater's unique power to free the self of its censor and to
make reality immediate. As influence or catalyst the theater can be
held to contribute something to the later novels; though none of
them have the underlying force to make the explosive moment,
their trend is to set scenes, to develop through dialogue, and the
guidebook descriptions of scenery give way to an outline a stage
artist could use.

In Jane Mander's London correspondent's column of the 1920's,
a note of passionate authority took over whenever theater was in
question; in Auckland in the 1930's she discussed in a radio talk the
little theatre movements she had been associated with. But New
Zealand in her lifetime was without the comparable experience
which might have helped it to respond to what she said and to see
the likely significance of her involvement in relation to her writing.

Local repertory was building itself up slowly on unprovocative plays with good boxoffice records. It is only in postwar years, and primarily through Wellington's Unity Theatre, that New Zealanders have discovered how the bold productions of dedicated groups, working in decrepit buildings, can fertilize the contiguous arts. By the time Jane Mander turned in 1934 to specific discussion of American influence, she was obsessed by the damage the language of the films could do to current writing: in the Christchurch *Press* she protested at her friend A. R. D. Fairburn's suggestion that "our writers could learn more from their counterparts in the colonial tradition in American letters, more from men like Mark Twain and the more modern Ernest Hemingway, than they could from such English writers as Mr. Galsworthy, Mr. Walpole, Mr. Aldous Huxley, and Mr. Priestley. And if it were only an attitude of mind to life and its material I should agree. But good writing means the fine use of our own language, and our language is English and not American." Then follows her prescription of Willa Cather as the only safe American model—a natural parallel, surely, to her advocacy of Henry Handel Richardson as the significant Australian.[20]

It is a curious and very incomplete answer to Mr. Fairburn's long and significant proposition, in which he suggested that "American literature may have a better influence on us than English, especially when we are considering contemporary writers. I know of no living English writer whose work I can read as a New Zealander. On the other hand there are several Americans who make me feel that I should be quite at home in the society they deal with: I should hate it but I should understand it. . . . And it is understanding, and not comfort, that we are seeking." Mr. Fairburn added his belief that "from the point of view of the New Zealand writer, 'Huckleberry Finn' is the most important novel ever written," and: "America . . . has falsified her destiny. Those who wince when I suggest that we should look to America must remember that the writers I have in mind have been, as colonial Americans, profoundly uncomfortable in cosmopolitan America, which is what we hear most about. Ernest Hemingway got out. But he is a true American, a colonial like ourselves, and closer to us than any Englishman."[21] Yet Jane Mander twice eulogizes Hemingway in her second *Press* article, first bracketing him with Katherine Mansfield as an artist in making small things significant, and then as "one of the coolest writers of the age. For a supreme example of what I am trying to explain I would

110	JANE MANDER

suggest the end of his 'Farewell to Arms.' Here the death of a girl
in childbirth after an idyllic love affair is presented with a severity
so apparently inhuman that it arouses the most violent emotions of
rage that life should treat the young and lovely in this manner . . .
exactly the reaction the author intended. A wonderful piece of work
this, but I tremble to think what the average New Zealand writer
would have made of it."

Her distress at Mr. Fairburn's thesis may be in part recoil from the
later part of his article where he deplores the hardening into Australian art of the unsuitable fashion of Swinburne and Beardsley: "This
fake-pagan Australian art has left imitation goat-tracks all over New
Zealand poetry and there are many older men who still live in the
world of the 'Triad.' But such cases of arrested development must
hold no interest for the young writer." Jane Mander had once loved
the *Triad* and those fashions very much, and one stays tender toward the first liberating influence. But these modes had persisted
in the antipodes for years after she had gone overseas; the direction
Mr. Fairburn prescribed was the one in fact taken now by New Zealand writers; and one might speculate that she had received and
turned to good account that "understanding, and not comfort, that
we are seeking," if not consciously through her reading, by the
privilege of living in America itself. *Allen Adair* had many signs of
a search for a casually endemic foothold, and if she had sat down in
1934 to another novel of the north, again bypassing cosmopolitan
strivings, she might have realized how close her literary practice was
to that of her younger New Zealand friends.

VII   *Local Forerunners*

Jane Mander's silence about the New Zealand fiction that preceded hers is understandable if we acknowledge the kind of ambition she had for it and for herself, as well as her toughly professional
attitude toward writing. Occasionally she had to write a survey in
which earlier novelists had claim to mention; then she mentioned
them. Given her own choice of subject she talked about overseas
books and the New Zealand writers of the 1930's; her references to
John A. Lee's *Children of the Poor* (1934) carry the implication that
"We're off at last." Always generous and ready to promote neglected books, she seems simply to have felt unrelated to earlier
New Zealand fiction. It was admittedly weak technically; the feminism that puts her in the same group as several predecessors is a

tenuous, nonliterary link. Robin Hyde, thirty years younger, considered Jane Mander a "modern," adding "age has nothing to do with it."[22]

The reticence about William Satchell is disappointing in that the two are paired nowadays as the first New Zealand novelists a nonspecialist need notice. Jane Mander reviewed *The Greenstone Door* on its reissue as a "faithful picture of the Maori life of the day . . . . The author is at his best with these native pictures, and in his description of the country. But when he goes to Auckland to Government House and Sir George Grey he falls into a conventional treatment of his characters, who are not as well individualised as the people of the bush."[23] Otherwise she is silent about him; yet *The Land of the Lost* must have been before her in Whangarei. How consciously, then, did she say in 1931, "Apparently no one else will ever be able to do that gum country of the north which is in my blood and bones"?[24]

If one sees her as almost exclusively concerned with human behavior, very sure that the twentieth century would illuminate it through science and psychology, uplift it by education and legislation, then of course she might not respond to Satchell's quiet, fatalistic view. In Satchell it is the landscape that is dynamic; man is in its presence. In Mark Gird, writes Phillip Wilson, "the author's mystique of the sacredness of the bush (briefly mentioned in *The Land of the Lost*) and the utu or price which its destruction entails, now finds explicit expression: 'Every bushman knows the toll demanded by the virgin forest. It is fixed and inexorable, and though skill in bushcraft will carry a man far in the avoidance of accidents, it counts for nothing when the time comes for the bush to demand its price.'"[25] When Jane Mander needs Tom Roland's death the bush is not the agent, though, all mystique apart, a falling tree is any bushman's likely end; it is self-determined by Tom who derails his logging trucks to avoid children playing on the line, thus keeping even death within the social context.

VIII *"The Most Guarded Treatment"*

"By what it shall decide to do in respect to the 'young' the great prose fable will, from any serious point of view, practically see itself stand or fall . . ." wrote Henry James. "While society was frank, was free about the incidents and accidents of the human constitution, the novel took the same robust ease as society. The young were then so very young that they were not table-high. But they began to grow and from the moment their little chins rested on the mahogany, Richardson and Fielding began to go under it. There came into being a mistrust of any but the most guarded treatment of the great relation between men and women, the constant world-renewal. . . ."[26] Jane Mander grew up in a society which had not only gone under the table, as it were, but had cut itself a hole through the floor and into the ground.

The immigrants had been able to leave behind them anything that related to the period of society's "robust ease" and were cut off from the reminders of it strewn through the arts of Europe. The anthropocentric view of creation arising out of Christianity, when confined by Victorian prudery, now saw the human constitution as more closely related to the angels than to any of earth's mammals. The settlers might not deny Darwin—within limits they were well educated and proud of it—but they knew how to dismiss him from their reckoning, handling their children so that they should never suspect kinship with any animal, too often depriving them of the animal's unconscious ease. How they maintained this attitude through life in tents and shacks is one of the miracles of colonization, explicable only by their ideal—the life possible in an upper-middle-class British home.

Struggling up out of this Jane Mander somehow reached a position where she could relate the physical to the emotional—giving the young their due place—so naturally as to appear out of the blue as a modern. This aspect of *The River* is without the dating assertiveness of some of its social theories. Asia is the protagonist, with her outspoken claims to be part of the human story, to be aware of much that goes on though they will not tell her. The descriptions of Asia as the attractive young woman the two Australians see—with her "bare legs," her "loosely poised body," "the freest body they had ever seen"—though gawky and unconvincing in execution, are a noble attempt to create a type that will move as if physically related to the place. But it is in her treatment of Alice's maladies and neurasthenia that Jane Mander most surely establishes herself: she so ties up the interaction of Alice's heart, mind, and body, notes the ups and downs so relevantly, yet decorously, that one wonders why it was ever thought good enough to cover a woman's predicament with a set of vaporous illnesses.

The first New Zealand novelist to try an honest reckoning with the human constitution, she was the last for a long time, if one excepts Jean Devanny's exploitation of it in *The Butcher Shop* (1926). As late as 1934 Jane Mander could still observe justly:

There has recently, as everyone knows, been a surfeit of "frankness," a reaction against the hypocritical mawkishness of the last century. But such frankness has hardly impinged upon New Zealand fiction. Our writers still proceed on the theory that we are some special sort of race that never has an indecent thought; and our insides might be made of plaster of paris for all the notice that is taken of them. And yet we all know that our insides have a tremendous effect on our thoughts, our motives and our actions, our struggles, our achievements, and our failures. It is the everlasting battle between mind and body that makes great drama. I am not suggesting that we try to imitate D. H. Lawrence; but great writers see the darkness as well as the light.[27]

In the later novels the reckoning is always there, if less strikingly; their themes have not perhaps the same need. It is a pity she narrowed her field to young adults and their aspirations, increasingly leaving out children, adolescents, and the mature and, except for *Allen Adair,* turning away from the long look at a family group. She continued to notice odd attitudes to the human constitution and to the young. One of her London columns to New Zealand newspapers was on stage censorship in 1927 when the Lord Chamberlain had suppressed within a year a Noel Coward, a Pirandello, a Eugene O'Neill, and "Young Woodley"—and a New York friend had written asking what on earth could be held to be wrong with the last one. The play, she commented,

has a love scene (but not one leading to seduction) between a schoolmaster's wife and a prefect . . . . There would be a fearful hullaballoo in England at the mere suggestion that masters' wives and public school boys ever met to kiss each other, just as much of a row as if somebody in America wrote a play picturing the President of the States with a negro mistress. Every country has its funny notions. I am quite willing to admit that one of the funniest is the English one that adolescents must be sheltered from all knowledge of the very thing that makes them adolescents.[28]

IX *The Climate of Taste*

The embellishments of New Zealand girlhood were gardening and music, the neopuritan woman's authorized panaceas: gardening the innocuous, and music the one art which can express without revealing what is expressed. The Manders made their brief gardens and moved on, but they never gave up. For music Jane Mander has said she used a cracked harmonium for the first years; she worked hard and later became a creditable pianist, with a leaning toward Beethoven like her women of *The River*. Houses were bare, boxes often served for furniture. It was a childhood she was intensely proud of and grateful for, but it was one that encouraged grandeur rather than finesse. The north was predisposed to make a virtue of its necessities, warding off the extras that might cultivate the senses, though often enough making stern sacrifice for formal education. There were a number of immigrants as individually developed as Mrs. Brayton, besides some quite extraordinary scholars and musicians, dotted through the north, and they had a long-term effect on youngsters in search of a distant goal. What they could not do was to alter the tenor of an environment where even in prosperity the arts were segregated and restricted as spare-time parlor accomplishments.[29]

Jane Mander and Katherine Mansfield, bracketed inevitably and fairly as the two of their time who had to leave their country to write, made strongly contrasting journeys toward the overseas life. Katherine Mansfield had a girlhood stay in England and in New Zealand lived within such gentleness and luxury as was to be had there. Jane Mander was thirty before she left the north for Sydney, her first encounter with people who explored various ways of living. One trophy of this experience is of course *The Strange Attraction*'s juxtaposition of the exotic Australian and the north: "All Dargaville knew that Dane lounged about like a woman on gorgeous cushions, that his rooms were filled with colour and scent. The pioneer spirit, conveniently recent enough to be quoted, was offended."

By the time she was thirty there was enough well-being in the local scene for some amelioration to be looked for; what hurt now was the absence of any sign that the ease would be used to good purpose. She could justifiably write:

When I left this country in 1912 I was entirely ignorant of art in painting, sculpture and architecture. Apart from some fine old furniture, books, prints and objets d'art we had not any art to mention in this country. And my roots were in that most trashy of all ages—the late Victorian era, with its bric-à-brac mind. I had an awful lot to get out of my system, and it took years of study and acquaintance with great work to train my taste. Music was the only art in which my taste was good.[30]

Insofar as she ever expressed or analyzed the situation, she saw it as a matter of going forward to cultivate taste through study and intellectual comprehension; yet as a novelist she went to the essence, pleading for the very climate of taste, the human leniency that allows the senses to expand to a practiced refinement. She took herself away into such climates too late to develop grace of style; yet if she had reached them in time, the impulse of her novels might have been quite other than the necessary revolt against the "thing in itself" of puritanism.

X *New Zealand Revisited*

After two years of reading the stories that struggled into print and the unprintable manuscripts thrust at her in Auckland, Jane Mander exploded: six long articles in the Christchurch *Press* late in 1934 tore up the current scene and offered a formula for rebuilding.[31] She found hundreds of scribblers, whom she called "The New Stupid," tempted to write for quick money or importance, none of them with as much promise as the comparable writers of thirty years earlier. Censuring local journals for buying from people who could never amount to anything, she went on to give standard advice on writing coolly, on rewriting, and on remembering that people were still people wherever one happened to set them down. As a reader for publishers she could speak authoritatively of what London, still the arbiter, required of suppliant manuscripts, and what was said there about rejected ones.

In the sixth article, subtitled "The Struggle Against Environment," the searchlight turns on the community: "What sort of collective stimulus does this country offer to its potential creative workers?" Twenty years earlier, when she first went to Columbia University, she was astonished to find herself regarded as an "event of importance." But now, "we have for the rest of the world today no ideas worth a tinker's cuss. We are afraid of new ideas. We forbid our citizens to go to countries that specialise in new ideas. We have, mentally and spiritually, I repeat in all seriousness, become one of the backward peoples of the earth." Responsible people had recently asked her in England what had come over her country. "When your women come here the only thing they can think about is being presented at Court, and all your men can talk about is the price of wool and butter and the scores of the All Blacks."

To starve the sense of beauty on any wide scale in any country is to invite
a whole crop of mental disorders. Already we have in this country an
amount of adult insanity that staggers visitors to our shores. It is not at all
puzzling to the psychologist who knows the deadly results of the psychic
starvation induced by the small town mind. . . . If this country doesn't mind
it will soon be known as the place where more adults go mad than in any
other place in the world, and we may achieve a new publicity as the world's
greatest madhouse. This is not a joke. There is more to escape from, spiritually speaking, in this country than in any place I have lived in.

She went on to demolish the idea that her country was too young,
its initial hardship too recent, for the development of taste. "In
fact our pioneering difficulties would make an Australian or a South
African grin. It is high time we stopped making them an excuse for
lack of taste." Most of all she deplored the betrayal of the trust left
by the "idealistic band of Englishmen who nursed us with fine
traditions and with protests against the stupidities of older countries." Through backsliding, New Zealanders had reached the point
where "when we ask what art it is that rouses enthusiasm in this
country the answer seems to be that for women it is cake-making,
and for men chest development."[32]
     The dimness of the New Zealand she had returned to is unde-
niable. Looking back, one can see the justice of her refusal to hold
economics entirely responsible for the sufferings of the depression,
and of her attack on another kind of poverty that had entrenched
itself during the monied 1920's. "I don't think, retrospectively, that
we reacted very well," wrote John Mulgan in 1945. "It was a source
of grief to many New Zealanders to find their spiritual resources
in quality well below their sunburnt and muscular bodies. . . . We
had lived as a community in a fair state of material happiness and
unconcern, and now the insubstantial nature of this living came
home to us."[33] With the Labour victory of 1935 Jane Mander could
see New Zealand on the move again with an idea or two; from 1938
on world affairs took precedence. The *Press* articles are her last major diatribe.
     Where her argument went astray was in crediting the pioneers
as a whole with the kind of vision that would lead to a developed
sense of beauty. The materialistic ordinariness she assailed is still
dominant, but it is now held only to be expected, given such origins.
A fierce desire to promote education and human rights was brought

here by immigrants who had had little responsibility for what is notably beautiful in their own country; these greatly outnumbered the few whose background was in any way equal to the situation. Pitchforked into one of the world's most austerely grand landscapes, the progressives of the British lower and middle classes domesticated it to the image of a minor suburbia. Nearly everyone had enough money and owned enough land to do his own bit of damage. What the state did—and state enterprise came early—was only a wider spreading of the same petty vision—and still is, as each new project town testifies. New Zealanders returning from overseas continue to be hit by the more than superficial mediocrity of what has been built in place of what was destroyed; the state of shock Jane Mander was in when she wrote these articles is a very familiar one.

XI *"No Background?"*

"Certainly our country life novels should give the flavour of this land, but not as something apart from the people who smell it and walk about its hills," Jane Mander wrote in the fifth *Press* article. "The great beauty of English novels of the soil and their everlasting appeal lie in the relation of the people of England to their land. . . . In a land of such varied beauty as New Zealand it is to be expected that a profound relation, even if inarticulate, should exist between human creatures and the earth." Although the articles do not refer to her own writing, either in plaint or pride, their awareness parallels every question we might ask about her books except perhaps the most pertinent: what is an author to do when her characters have not yet attained a relationship with the land?

The first northern settlers, the adults fictionally explored in *The River*, felt mostly hostility, unease, or indifference to the country as they found it. Acceptance came slowly, with conversion and domestication—the more slowly in that immigrants were all from one country and so did not have to build up the local environment as a common frame of reference as immigrants of mixed origin are impelled to do. It is estimated that New Zealand is considerably slower than the United States—or even than Australia—at turning its immigrants into natives.

The River and *Allen Adair* illustrate the tentative beginnings of this relation of incomers to new surroundings; neither book has quite the technique for a proposition where nothing at all can be assumed about any part of the setting, or anyone's relation to it, where everything must be defined in one way or another. One result is what now reads as overemphasis in Allen Adair's bond with the gumfield; if it were an English moor it would be so rich in context and association that allusion would suffice. The inept scenic descriptions of *The River*'s first chapter seem to be born of the author's uncertainty as to who is looking at the scenery, and how familiarly.

The experience of another New Zealand novelist is useful to consider on this crucial point. Adding to what Jane Mander had said, Ngaio Marsh—also in the *Press*—pointed out: "It is when she deals with the technical problems of the New Zealand novel that I find her most enthralling. Among many others I have tried to write such a novel and have found myself confronted by difficulties as great as they are hard to define." She instanced the painter in oils, who must paint background and the emerging figures at the same time; wherever the background and figures touch, both must be wet. "Such, I believe, is the problem of the New Zealand novel. . . . There can be no help at all in the construction of a careful mise en scène, overloaded with local colour, unless the characters grow out of it and live in front of it. Even then they may be embarrassed and made foolish by their surroundings." Ngaio Marsh went on to say:

It seems to me that in this country we do not yet grow out of our surroundings. Perhaps this is because we have had, as Miss Mander points out, a relatively easy colonisation. We are transplanted English. We move across the surface of this country, we super-impose our racial habit upon a dry background. We have no national architecture. Our houses are English homes adapted unwillingly to the exigencies of the climate. We have no national school of painting. Our painters follow one or another of the European methods. This is reasonable enough. It is no good trying to force an individual art or to reconcile things that are, at the moment irreconcilable.

Is this situation matter in itself for a novel, "No Background?" In England, perhaps a little under the influence of nostalgia, I began to think so. I wrote the opening chapters of a novel in a New Zealand setting. For a time it seemed to me that the background and figures worked well together, the one growing up out of the other without too much insistence on either. Then, after an interval, I read what I had written and at once realised that it would not do. Already I had lost my first intention and was steaming off busily down the well-worn rails of the colonial novel. I had merely changed the landscape and might as well have sent my characters to

Canada or Jericho. Gone was the idea which was to have been the whole matter of my book. I turned, more successfully, to crime fiction. . . .[34]

Up to a point, Jane Mander had no problem of communication with the whole English-speaking world. The dialogue is standard English, and the principals chosen are such that the author can "melt . . . narrative into the thought processes (and personal idiom) of the characters," as R. A. Copland puts it. He points out also that "By no outrage against the New Zealand realities the school-teacher can be reasonably well educated and yet almost fully immersed in the common life whether of country or town. . . . If a list were compiled of New Zealand fiction in which a teacher or a student has been the means for reconciling 'medium and message' the list would contain work by many of our best writers."[35] The school-teacher, or someone akin, which Jane Mander's own experience comprehended, suited the circumstances very well; at their best the journeys in and out of the authorial viewpoint are deft sorties at the end of a short rope, refraining from presumptuous plunges into minds of distant origin; the latter are left to observation and their own speech.

Where the communicative ability failed was in describing the outdoor world; if the more obvious blunders are any guide, the cause was Jane Mander's unsureness of who her audience was, except that it must not be less than the whole world at the outset. Most of the faults of *The River*—the novel where both achievement and mistake reach their maximum—come from ambition to write an epic with a full set of stage props, and because nobody outside a few thousand northerners knew what their country looked like, it must be fully painted in—mixed bush, kauri forest, gumfield and all. Her ardor trips her in the first chapter in this notorious passage:

There was a riotous spring colour in the forest, voluptuous gold and red in the clumps of yellow kowhai and crimson rata, and there were masses of greeny white clematis and bowers of pale tree ferns to rest the satiated eye. Stiff laurel-like puriris stood beside the drooping fringe of the lacy rimu; hard blackish kahikateas brooded over the oak-like ti-toki with its lovely scarlet berry.

"What picture can that possibly convey to an English reader?" asked Katherine Mansfield, and Professor Stevens, putting that question in its place, more pertinently asks: "is this bit of native, local information relevant to the theme, significant, and contributing to the total effect? What is Jane Mander wanting to do? To convey Alice's state of mind? (Did *Alice* know the Maori names?) To make a picture for us? Or has she been betrayed into what is merely a pointless tourist blurb? The latter, I believe."[36]

The human drama developing very nicely during the river journey in the minds of Alice, David, and Asia is interrupted by the author— as by a guide with a megaphone—under a multiplicity of pressures from the amorphous unknown readership. Novels have scenic descriptions, and New Zealand has the scenery (if nothing else, the world has often implied). One suspects that the descriptive passages did speciously help launch the book at first; several reviewers chose to commend the next passage:

Towering arrogantly above all else, on the crests and down the spurs, stood‧ groups of the kauri, the giant timber tree of New Zealand, whose great grey trunks, like the pillars in the ancient halls of Karnak, shot up seventy and eighty feet without a knot or branch. . . .

If Jane Mander could have trusted the world to be interested in her people, or if she could have held in her heart as she wrote one responsive group of compatriots to whom mere allusion to the external view would have sufficed, she need not have been betrayed into an undertaking so foreign to her talent. In *Allen Adair* high-flying is renounced; there is disappointment now, taken inwardly—nobody wants another New Zealand book, but the book asks to be written, and the result is harmonious. The last two novels are aimed at a reduced but specific audience overseas.

It is a commonplace now that New Zealand writers were stranded for some decades without a sense of audience—in the period when they had ceased to be English immigrants writing for the English and were not yet New Zealanders transmitting to compatriots. Jane Mander fell into these empty times when the trouble was scarcely recognized. Her alliance with human fundamentals carried her through; her lapses were spasmodic and superficial, but they are very obvious because her ear which was sharp enough for the spoken word was otherwise dull. This is the defect that makes her small writings uncongenial and less quotable than their content sometimes merits, but it is most obtrusive when she tries to pin down overwhelming beauty. One might attribute the defect partly to the neopuritan ban on the exercise of sensibility: emerging from such a background one can throw off the shackles only to be caught out as unpracticed in finer shadings and restraint. Whatever the cause, she is inherently short of the poet's precision with words and images; she is merely accurate.

The passage from *The River* quoted above, which has helped brand her as an indifferent botanist, is scientifically defensible, oddly enough: the brief seasons of clematis and kowhai do usually coincide, rata pleases itself, and the ti-toki berries would have hung on through the winter. Similarly with the concerted riot of spring and summer flowers in Mrs. Brayton's garden a few days later: flowers are thoroughly bewildered by the north's indeterminate seasons; anything can happen. Yet one shrinks from these passages as essentially untruthful; they are a little distorted by an unconscious tilting toward an overseas audience receptive of marvels. At the time she wrote, Jane Mander would have needed a lot of nerve to leave out scenic description. As late as 1934 Ngaio Marsh offered an alternative only as a speculative counsel of perfection: "I believe that it is only by the practice of the most stringent austerity of style that we have any hope of achievement. It also seems to me that the landscape can be felt only through the spiritual and mental experiences of human beings. If these are realised it may be that the shapes of mountains and rivers will appear, not as so many theatrical properties, but inevitably, so that the story could have unfolded in no other setting."[37]

XII   *Hand-forged*

While the New Zealand background resisted the novelist's need to merge and assimilate it, the human figures had a recalcitrance all their own, summed up by Robert Chapman in 1953:

> One of the main difficulties . . . which confines the approaches possible to those who write and set their fiction in New Zealand is the absence here of widely recognised psychological stereotypes. The squire, the parson, the cultured aristocrat, the Birmingham businessman, the clerk with white collar and umbrella, the spiv or the Cockney, just have not got established local equivalents. This has many effects. It makes it difficult, if not impossible, to use the ordinary lending-library-romance technique of sketching a few of the outlines of an attractive or villainous stereotype and allowing the reader to do the rest with his emotionally positive stock picture. . . .

Stereotypes are not wholly wrong but rather the highest common factor of general observation in a stable pattern. Where the pattern has not been stable for long enough nor been sufficiently stratified and geographically various to provide a variety of stereotypes, the consequence for the serious writer is that he cannot touch in any of his characters lightly or make them begin to live by showing one or two exactly observed departures from the expected norm. Each character must be handwrought. . . .[38]

Jane Mander forged her characters by hand; hers are the first New Zealand novels to be built successfully on this principle, and for a long time they were the only ones. Some of her characters—Mrs. Brayton, for instance, and Dick Rossiter and Mrs. Dubbins—are stereotypes in that they have come to New Zealand already shaped by recognizable molds of nineteenth-century Britain. Every community had such people, which a novelist must use to remain probable; but these in New Zealand novels are like characters borrowed, costumes and all, from one play which they know well, and thrown into a completely strange one in which they must somehow involve themselves. They may stride into a leading role or stand aside commenting; either way they are usable. What matters is the credibility of the new play, its projection of the forces which will finally make a new set of stereotypes, altering or throwing out the imported ones in the process.

The social mechanism of Jane Mander's small communities was a very strong one; she understood it acutely. Their complex intimacy, enforced neighborliness irrespective of status, and shared commitment to an ill-defined experiment were blunting the outlines of the imported patterns. Nobody could walk onto the stage and off it without changing and being changed by the rest of the cast. The author's truth about the community is contingent on her demonstrating the importance of each individual. Sometimes for want of space or technique she falls short of investing a lesser individual with a whole personality; even so we can sense the intention, the avoidance of routine. Some of the angularity of her novels comes from this very unwillingness to give a character a distant nod and move on; she will keep a person on stage to scold when we feel that a quiet dismissal would be as effective. This awkwardness comes from the same source as her strength, from the tenets of frontier society where a merely casual greeting can be an insult, and a reprimand less hurtful than a brushoff.

In shaping her New Zealand characters she had no help at all from precedent. Tom Roland, an adult in the 1880's, is of the small first generation of New Zealand-born. Even if a type could be said to have established itself already, it is without literary relative. Yet he is brilliantly credible. He springs straight out of the native soil and could properly claim to be the first convincing New Zealander in fiction. Allen Adair and Jack Ridgefield, who is of a later generation, are another style of native—men embedded in their environment, serving rather than using it. These two normal men are recognizably of an ideal national type that has since become accepted: the strong, shy, backblocks Kiwi whom everyone leans on. To have the proto-type pinned down in a book before nature has had time to run off its copies is, of course, the mark of a good novelist.

The bush communities that provided Jane Mander's material had also largely defined the way she should use it. The shaping of her viewpoint is explicit in an article of 1928 where she contrasts her London life with her childhood:

> To most Londoners death is so familiar a thing that it loses significance. But I still shrink from the thought that people are dying round me in large numbers every day. In our small forest community any death was a catas-trophe that upset us for weeks. For we had no old people, no useless people, and even the more ordinary individual had remarkable value; had, in fact, a sort of grandeur, because he could deal with fires and storms and floods, and might make all the difference between safety and disaster.
>
> If a person left us suddenly it was almost as bad as death, for it often took months to fill the gap. The coming of new people gave us an additional sense of security. They meant more hands, and in the bush hands are worth more than brains.
>
> So I grew up to think people tremendously important, even the people one did not like. The difference in the estimate of neighbours is amusing. Neighbours were sacred in the forest. . . .[39]

When tested against her practice, this is found to be an accurate analysis: sparse, interdependent peopling is structural in her New Zealand novels. *The River*'s first lesson is that Alice cannot throw off the consequences of having treated David like a disreputable cab driver whom she could pay off at the end of the trip. The moral is not that she was mistaken about him but that she had left behind choice and its manifestations when she came to where people were tremendously important, even "the people one did not like." A sunnier version of the theme occurs in *Allen Adair* when Pahi sights the river boat:

Indeed, the cry had gone forth to every corner of the village, and there was not a soul in the place who did not see Allen landed all by himself at the end of the long wooden wharf with his carpet bag and portmanteau, while the tug puffed on round the bend.

Pahi was one of the many places in the north in those days where the newcomer was an asset. Even if he only came to be a nuisance he was an excitement. If he came merely to be agreeable he was a party. If he came to work he was a godsend. If he came to spend money he was a bank. The women on the Horton verandah rather hoped he would be the party. There were so few people who were like parties. The pub owner and the storeman hoped he would be the bank. The two farmers in the store hoped he was looking for work. The rest of the inhabitants were thankful that he was an incident, and that they could ask Old Tom's daughter, the gossipy postmistress in the store branch, what she had learned about him.

XIII *Do They Speak English out There?*

The dialogue of these novels, held to have done "much to set New Zealand fiction on the road of naturalism in talk,"[40] is a long jump ahead of the set literary speeches of earlier fiction and can be taken as an index of the way talk went among the kind of people portrayed. The British-born principals—Alice Roland, David Bruce, and Mrs. Brayton; Dick Rossiter and Arthur Devereux—are of the educated class, speaking as they did at home in England. With them might be put the cosmopolitan Australian journalist, Dane Barrington, whose speech would have no inducement to use any of the embryonic forms of "Strine" he might put in his articles. In another immigrant class we have the unmitigated dialects of Mrs. Lyman: "It was me 'e wanted, not 'er, and 'e would 'ave married me if 'e could 'ave got a divorce from 'er"; and Mrs. Dubbins: "Takin' the liberty, ma'am, I've brought yer a little of the best, thinkin' as 'ow yer mightn't 'ave any, and me that 'shamed of Dubbins, as is in no state to 'elp, ma'am, and it will 'elp yer like nothin' else, as I've found mesself in me troubles." Alongside are the native-born: except for Asia, whose models are her mother, David and Mrs. Brayton, the young New Zealand principals have had fairly long formal education which would set the standard English they speak. Tom Roland deviates, but his "ain't" and "she don't" are a relic of immigrant dialect, not a New Zealand one. Moreover, he is old enough to have missed state education.

The first impact of New Zealand education was to level up speech, removing grosser errors of grammar and pronunciation. Mrs. Gird in Satchell's *The Toll of the Bush* witnesses at the turn of the century:

You must not be surprised at poor people speaking good English: we are a very long way ahead of your countrymen in that respect you know. Your people are handicapped by the fact that they have lived for hundreds of years in small communities, hence the language has been broken up into innumerable dialects. Our facilities for communication, on the other hand, enable us to speak one language, and our educational system ensures that that language shall be the best.[41]

Later a New Zealand accent, phonetically measurable, was operating at least by the era Jane Mander's second and third novels are set in; its trend has been attributed to the number of Londoners among early schoolteachers.[42] Thus while the majority improved, the upper-class immigrants found their children's speech descending some distance from their own towards a norm—a process hastened by everybody's reluctance to sound like a toff. But there was very little for a novelist to transcribe.

Ambiguous and inhibiting pressures have molded by now a characteristic New Zealand speech; part of these novels' modernity is their accurate styling of the beginnings, which keeps them within the framework of what has in fact happened since. For several generations New Zealand girls have tended to speak so much more correctly and fluently than their brothers that they can appear to have been born some castes higher. It pays a girl to improve herself; it pays a boy to give a tough impression, speaking carelessly and as briefly as possible. Jane Mander's novels have no eloquent Kiwi males, but they provide an overseas man for every bright young woman who likes to converse with a man, and for Alice Roland there is David.

Allen Adair has neither woman with inquiring mind nor overseas man (except Dick who is too furtive to talk); in the silence a number of minor characters are heard, shortly but quite distinctly. Allen himself is under intangible pressure to reduce speech to the scale of the men around him which he is happy to do; Peter Horton manages with even fewer words; Allen's father and sundry other men are laconic indeed. Their vocabulary is minimal: here begins the Kiwi code that bars any word conceivably puzzling to the hearer. It is

totally uninventive—again true to local style which has never
sported with language in Australian fashion. Adding Tom Roland's
condensed, functional speech and Jack Ridgefield's short, correct
sentences, we have the pattern of the men of influence, the trend-
setters, very close to the modern male idiom. Yet Allen is word
sensitive; Marion's usages grate on him, and one can detect some
uneasy gentility in her correctness. She is at sea between Allen, who
could use the language if he would, and the honest idiom of her
mother: "My nearest neighbour was ten miles away at first, and only
men at that, and when it came to my time with the first there wasn't
anybody to get regular, and it came unexpected, too." *Allen Adair*
is the most interesting conversation piece among the novels, captur-
ing what little there was to get hold of at that stage.

"Before I left London," Jane Mander wrote in 1934, "I was asked
by a publisher who gets a good many scripts from New Zealand,
'Don't people speak English out there? . . . The conversations I get
in these novels are so extraordinary, a kind of doggerel, as if people
were generally illiterate.' From my own experience of scripts sent
me I can confirm this surprising statement." She went on to remark
on New Zealand's general education and its pride in having
removed class distinction from speech. "Yet when our writers come
to deal with it, we have a composite lingo like nothing on
earth. . . . And in the books about old times anachronisms of
gangster slang mingle with Victorian quaintness . . . about my
father's mills and camps there came and went as tough and as varied
a lot of men as could be found anywhere; but they did not talk like
the American film. They spoke robust, simple English, or Scotch or
Irish or cockney or county dialect or Oxford. And if our writers
cannot reproduce these varieties of speech they had better write the
simplest English they know of, that of the Bible."[43]

Jane Mander owed her literacy to her gentle mother and to the
Kerr family's hold on books and on self-education, but the ability to
feel and write as a New Zealander she may have owed in part to her
father's want of education. Very few of his generation had such a
sense of identity with the country. He went about the land using it,
altering it, dreaming for it, totally and unquestioningly investing
himself and his heirs. Almost unschooled, and little influenced by
books, he had been self-supporting so young that he was somewhat
outside the pressure of his parents' nostalgia for England. He knew
he spoke badly—this bothered him and he set about to improve

when he stood for Parliament—but the way he spoke had worked well in what he had to do. In all the capabilities by which a frontiersman was judged he outdid the men around him.

The sense of belonging to and of possessing their country, which New Zealanders have been very slow to attain, came first to the less educated. The more a family made books a part of life, the more its mind was divided between the local reality and the equally powerful reality of literature, particularly that of England. The ambition of all advanced students of Jane Mander's day was to take a degree at one of the great British universities; grooming for this began young. She might not have been a New Zealand novelist if a turn in her father's fortunes had put her into the mainstream of academic life in Auckland, where she appeared to belong. By the time she went she was too assuredly a New Zealander to change herself fundamentally; she had had that much longer to reinforce herself with her father's confidence, the more effectively in that she had to contend with him to get away at all.

CHAPTER 6

Impact and Reverberation

HAPPY and acclimatized though Jane Mander was overseas, her talent was liable to draw precariously on its reserves, as it needed one hemisphere for its flowering and the other for its radical nourishment. As a pioneer expatriate writer, she was very much alone in the dilemma—then scarcely recognized—which Janet Frame has recently defined:

> If a writer lives in exile and writes forever of his native land his work may fail to develop and mature, or it may be restricted to a narrow period of memory. If he's a genius he may get away with it: nostalgia plus obsession plus technique are fair qualifications for a writer. In exile which he or others may be deceived into describing as "self-imposed," when it may be imposed as strongly though invisibly by the society of his land as if it had been forced exile from a totalitarian state, he finds his themes in his adopted land; but his work may suffer.[1]

There are indeed degrees of exile, determined by what the home country would do, if it could, to make exile unnecessary. With only one million people, spread thin over a long, wild terrain, New Zealand could not then hope to support its major artists, any more than it could an Ernest Rutherford or the many other specialists whose abilities were claimed and held by international centers. The expatriate, though, longing for some basis of living and working back home, would often subject New Zealand to brooding appraisal: was its inability to provide for him due to smallness of stature or smallness of spirit? Nobody could get a straighter verdict on this than a novelist: books could go everywhere, straight to the hands of any literate individual who cared (and almost all New Zealanders were literate). A book's reception was as clear an answer as a referendum. Taking into account the whittled royalties on colonial editions, considerable success among New Zealand's one million might only have kept Jane Mander in typing paper. But that was scarcely the point, for token appreciation from the right quarter has infinite sustaining power. Rejection from the home quarter could be as disproportionately damaging; Jane Mander had to come to terms somehow with her country's unequivocal reply that it would not support her if it could.

Almost certainly she was unprepared for the rebuff; she knew that her progressive frontier society still lacked the arts, but she appears to have credited it with a spirit as eager as her own to supply the deficiency. It was in her nature to give others the benefit of the doubt. She was quite out of touch with the current actuality and indeed had no way of testing it: those aspects of New Zealand which the admiration of her New York friends kept burnished for her—its record as a utopia, its heroic contribution to the 1914-18 war—prevented her seeing that in ways that were to affect her vitally her country had become strangely sick.[2] Not that any awareness might have saved her, if one can argue from the case of Frances Hodgkins who all this time was testing New Zealand's inflexibility against every inch of her progress. Frances Hodgkins grew up within New Zealand's culturally dominant southern centers, offered them her work in every phase, even returning twice from Europe to see what was possible; she found that severance came with every step she took away from their drawing-room expectations of painting toward a significant idiom: they would not budge. Jane Mander, though, had been developing unnoticed, as a novelist may; she had no writing of relevance to offer publicly until her first—and best—novel, when she was forty-three. She had dedicated it to her mother, and she posted off her mother's copy with the inscription: "At last—and such as it is."

Overseas reviews of *The River* were encouraging; critics noted the strengths as well as the stumblings; in the United States and Australia they were openly pleased to read about a little-known country. The *New York Times*, the *New Republic*, and the *Sydney Mail* featured it; the *San Francisco Bulletin*, the *Boston Transcript*, and Katherine Mansfield in the *Athenaeum* considered it at length.

New Zealand newspapers for the most part swept it under the carpet, having no precedents for judging local literature. The *New Zealand Herald*, the Auckland morning paper, in 350 words under a very small heading wrote sensibly enough: "What matters most—whether or not one accepts Miss Mander's challenge—is that this is a real novel, written of a real New Zealand, which can enter the lists in any large reading town of the world and command attention." The reservation is unstressed: "It is a weakness, one thinks, that a girl of eighteen should solve her love problem as she does— the standard of decision is too early for good public morality."[3] The *Dominion*, a Wellington newspaper, in brief but quite enthusiastic treatment gently sounded the notes that were to prevail for the decade: "The author . . . by the way is the daughter of a much-respected member of the New Zealand Parliament. . . . Her novel comes under the category of 'sex-problem' fiction."[4]

In Whangarei, the home town, *The River* went on the Public Library's discretionary list, to be lent only to approved adults who made special application; it stayed on the "Reserved" shelf in the librarian's private room with *Tess of the d'Urbervilles* and *The Water Gypsies*.[5] In Port Albert a subscriber took it upon herself to withdraw it as unfit, present residents skeptically recall. Other northerners testify that the book was kept from them as youngsters, to be handed over when they were "old enough." But the north had the peculiar and personal difficulty of its respect for the Mander family; embarrassment was in the air, and it was too decent to want to draw in the young. The northern "censorship" was a special case.

Most well-read youngsters of the day grew up without hearing of *The River* simply because New Zealand literature was outside consideration. University entrance scholarships, even degrees in English, went through in that decade without reference to New Zealand books. The few who were conscious of a need for their own regional literature were still too few to be effective; the forces against a book did not have to be strong to finish it. Between distaste and indifference—in proportions impossible now to determine —*The River* was lost.

The unspoken difficulty was that Jane Mander had written a story in which the reading public might see parallels between the principals and her family. Knowing as a novelist that the family setting had been only a starting point for her imagination, she did not foresee the literal identifications New Zealand readers would make—a habit of theirs which was to hound succeeding novelists into putting fictitious names to the towns of their stories and into other furtive devices. As late as 1961 the *New Zealand Listener* was forced by a naïve correspondent into editorial defense of writers:

People often dislike a story and write to say what they think is wrong with it. At such times we are always interested to notice how many readers want to discuss stories as if they were factual narratives. . . . Our pragmatic temper reveals itself in a reluctance to make any concession to fancy. Artistic effect, which must be the writer's aim, is disregarded. Writers are judged, again and again, on questions of fact which for them are of secondary importance or barely relevant.[6]

That some of the facts of *The River* were literally true naturally confused unsophisticated readers and played into the hands of the unsympathetic. The place names were all real: Kaiwaka showed on the map; Point Curtis was a tiny headland with wharf and pub—just as in the book—in use for those few years of milling. Therefore Tom Roland must be Frank Mander; it was not too implausible that Asia was Jane Mander, and how much of the rest might not be "true"? Looking at the story this way we can see how dreadful the implications could be. If there had been any previous experience of the impact of a realistic novel about a small New Zealand area, Jane Mander could have seen how it might be construed and given camouflage. If she had stayed in her own country to write, she must have been aware of how it would read there—so much so that the book would probably not have amounted to anything. We owe its creative strength to the freedom New York gave her to be a novelist. But if the result was to bring soreness where she hoped it would be only the cause of pride, the wound, in the long run, may have been greatest of all to herself. If her innocent spontaneity had misfired, could she allow it to recharge itself?

We do not know how soon repercussions reached the author. Mails were slow; it took about a month each way for letters, longer for parcels of books. New Zealand booksellers tended to wait for the English edition (which was some months later in this case) and to "wait and see" on principle before ordering a book with a New Zealand setting.[7] Knowledge of the reception would creep in slowly; the second novel was almost certainly in the press and the third one at least drafted before Jane Mander would have a real idea of the reckoning in New Zealand.

Reviews of *The Passionate Puritan* the next year ranged from a full page in the *New York Times Book Review*, attractively though incongruously illustrated with photos of Milford Sound and of Rotorua Maoris dancing to welcome the Prince of Wales,[8] to three inches of admonition in the *New Zealand Herald*, ending: "Has not the sex problem become somewhat of an obsession with many modern novelists? Jane Mander's description of the bush fire and of the men who fought it, is fine. This kind of thing we really look for in New Zealand fiction." The Wellington morning paper said reasonably enough that it was not up to her previous book and concluded, six inches later: "It is a pity Miss Mander does not give us a story of New Zealand country life, which would be free from the sex problem motif which has been over-prominent in the present story and its predecessor."[9] She was now doomed in New Zealand by being named as a sex-problem specialist. The word "sex" was itself to be avoided in conversation; classrooms of teen-aged girls would blush if it turned up in a botany lesson, and teachers went to much trouble to avoid it.

When *The Strange Attraction* arrived the next year, reviewers consolidated the old positions: the Americans found points to criticize in the writing but were pleased to read about a strange place; the British took the writing seriously, for better or worse, but were unenthusiastic about the setting; New Zealand reviewers kept to morality:

One can have nothing but the highest praise for the use she makes of the inanimate material she has at her disposal. The *Post's* London correspondent regrets the combination of what one may call the "sex" novel and the New Zealand bush country as unnecessary and misleading. (*Evening Post*, Wellington.)[10]

It is a great pity that Miss Jane Mander, the New Zealand novelist whose first story, "A New Zealand River," was so well reviewed both in London and New York, should continue to be so obsessed by sex problems. (The *Dominion*, Wellington.)[11]

It is somewhat unfortunate that Miss Mander's heroine is so determined to confuse the "freedom" of woman with a much older profession. Nor is it complimentary to the New Zealand girl, that what other readers may be led into thinking is a typical Aucklander, should punctuate her conversation with "Hell," should drink beer (though Miss Mander carefully terms it "ale") in the dining room of a rough country hotel, not because she particularly likes it, one feels sure, but merely to emphasise her distinction from what she would call "wowsers"—in short, an out-and-out pose! This Remuera girl (why this hit at Remuera in particular?). . . . (*New Zealand Herald*.)[12]

The *Auckland Star*, quite out of step, found enough good for a kindly column and a half.[13] But if a novel is reckoned to have undesirable aspects, its innocuous pages will not save it; and once again the author was evilly served by the dustjacket—still to be seen with the Alexander Turnbull Library's copy—which even overseas reviewers castigated for its lurid and repellent blonde. Jane Mander replied at last, in a letter from London to the *Auckland Star*:

As you were interested enough to publish the most impersonal review I have yet seen from the New Zealand Press of my third novel, and one that gave unusually representative quotations, I ask space to reply through your columns to some of the remarks of my New Zealand critics.

I really cannot understand why some of them call me sex-obsessed. Am I being compared out there with the publications of the Religious Tract Society? If I am being compared, as I should be, with the modern novel writers on this side of the world, that term cannot truthfully be applied to me. As a matter of fact I'm not half sexy enough for hundreds of thousands of readers here. The people who read my books here read them for the New Zealand colour, and certainly not for the sex element. I can think of only one review I have seen in the Old World that used the term in connection with my work. . . .

It is ironically true that her books are "not half sexy enough" for popularity in that their love interest is inherently unmoving, being mind-dominated and calculating sometimes to the point of incredibility; because of the strongly supporting social context of these affairs, readers can suppress some of their impatience with the love interest per se. Professional reviewers of the Old World were not likely to confuse theme and treatment, but in New Zealand they pounced on the word, as censors do. "I'm going to keep on believing," Jane Mander continued, "that my native land is producing about the same number of intelligent adults per thousand of the population as any other British country. It is unfortunate that the general newspaper has to be run for the average person, but at least the average person need not be misinformed."

I have been accused of putting into my third book characters who are "unrepresentative" of the community in which they are placed. Now a writer who is trying to be an artist, as I sincerely am, has nothing whatever to do with being a tourist agent, or a photographer, or a historian, or a compiler of community statistics. The question for critics is, not did two such people as Valerie Carr and Dane Barrington ever actually live in Dargaville, but might they have lived there? And the answer is that exceptional people may be found anywhere. And even if it has to be a question of fact, anyone who ever lived in the North of New Zealand for many years, as I did, must have been struck over and over again, by finding the most unlikely people in out-of-the-way places. If there was one thing significant about our North it was just that. I could not begin to put into books all the "unrepresentative" people we came across in the bushes, about the gum-fields, and in the small towns. . . .

But I can assure my critics I am not "hitting" at anything. . . . Nobody knows better than I that I have a lot to learn, and . . . that to be an artist one must not be petty. . . . Nobody who reads my books here will suppose that Dargaville is any different from the countless small towns all over the world, or that the fashionable suburb of Remuera is any worse than any other fashionable suburb simply because my unconventional character came out of it. Really we writers are not taken as literally as all that.

And, furthermore, I am not trying to shock anybody. I am writing to please myself, without any thought as to whether I am pleasing or annoying or shocking anybody else. If an artist stops to consider any section of his public, or what his friends would like, or what his publisher would like, or anything at all but that inner light inside himself, he ceases to be an artist and becomes a purveyor of goods. Unfortunately there are too many pur-veyors of goods trying to masquerade as artists in the world today. I am simply trying to be honest and to be loyal to my own experience.[14]

Eighteen months later the *London Mercury* carried a brief survey of New Zealand literature from Alan Mulgan in Auckland with this conclusion:

New Zealand literature, however, cannot live wholly in the past. The work of the living proceeds, amid many difficulties; Miss Mander has written three novels of New Zealand life and is writing a fourth. She announces, however, that if she does not get more encouragement from her own coun-try, she will write no more about it. In some candid counsel to New Zea-landers who aspire to London success, she says . . . that although she is sup-posed to have had a considerable literary success in England and America, and has enjoyed a good Press, she is today hundreds of pounds to the bad. . . . Perhaps Miss Rosemary Rees, whose *Heather of the South* has been run-ning serially in New Zealand, will be more successful financially. This is a more conventional and less ambitious novel than those of Miss Mander, and has that pleasantness of romance and unclouded happiness of ending (be-sides some excellent local colour) which the average New Zealander, not differing in this respect from other British publics, prefers.[15]

Jane Mander's "candid counsel" had been a column in New Zealand papers urging young artists to stay away from London unless they had a safe occupation or money to fall back on; unembittered as always, and conceding that writers are better off than painters or musicians, she lays it down in terms of rent and royalties what "considerable success" such as hers adds up to. "Then, on the colonial sale, we writers get threepence a copy. Calculate again how many copies we must sell to our sceptical or admiring compatriots before we make £10 out of those who should be proud to shake us by the hand."[16] Printings of her novels had been up to two thousand copies in America and England; she can scarcely have made £10 out of any of them in New Zealand. The unprovocative *Allen Adair* in 1925 did little for her. Two or three approved writers of "pleasantness" continued to flourish, and in 1926 Jean Devanny's first novel, *The Butcher Shop*, offered a formula for successful unpleasantness. This book gallops along with a violent sensuality which can still strike one as wilfully outrageous. The New Zealand board of censors banned it; the author reported her publishers delighted with its sales which reached fifteen thousand.

The only readers Jane Mander and Jean Devanny have in common are those who set themselves to read New Zealand fiction right through, but these authors shared the experience of testing local reaction to the idea that life in their country was less smooth than the carefully protected public image of it. The unsmiling belief in placid progress would admit no eccentricity, somber or gay. Confused and humbled by the depression of the 1930's, New Zealanders came at last to countenance various versions of their society—with protective gasps at first—but by the 1960's open to the implications of Janet Frame, Sylvia Ashton-Warner, and Ian Cross. New Zealand novels have in fact run ahead of the prediction made by Robin Hyde (who hailed Jane Mander as a "modern") that "they won't be surface compilations of the cheerful commonplaces of life."

I venture to make this prophecy. The best New Zealand literary work written in the next fifty years will bear the stamp of oddity. This is because, whether you like it or not, New Zealand is an extremely odd place, and the tenement of moody spirits. Look out for them when they get going.[17]

The New Zealand Jane Mander returned to in 1932 knew vaguely that she had been controversial but would have been hard put to it to say what she had written. The novels were not in evidence; the legend itself was already distorted: a long survey of New Zealand literature in *The Bookman* in February, 1930, said that "receiving scant support from her own people, she left for America with the avowed intention of writing no more of New Zealand. With her departure it may be said that there are none now writing novels of New Zealand life." Her presence in Auckland possibly aroused some interest in her books, but the country's changing temper probably had more to do with it; neither trend can have seemed very marked to the aging and unproductive author, and the major improvement in the country's disposition—an almost explosive movement toward liberation, diversity, and identity—began later, about the year of her death. By 1938 there was just enough persistent demand for *The River* to embolden her to arrange its reissue by other publishers, one of them in New Zealand.

Reviewing was now in the hands of professional writers: Frank Sargeson in the *Auckland Star*, and, in the South, C. R. Allen in the *Otago Daily Times* and M. H. Holcroft in the Christchurch *Press* all had space for proper appraisal. By 1960 another edition was needed, and here the State Literary Fund came forward to bridge the gap between high publishing costs and small population. It was on most college reading lists by this time, quite widely known and oddly at ease among recent novels; only the dates and an occasional long memory drew attention to the solitariness of its first appearance. *The River* had become the book against which phases of New Zealand's literary awareness could be measured.

The old attitude and the new met for one more duel in the *New Zealand Listener* in 1955, when a correspondent complained about the Gillespie Radio Portrait:

> Miss Mander appears to have been a forthright woman, but the world is full of forthright women and unfortunately full also of women, who, thinking they have a greater brain than their sisters, write books. If the BBC made programmes on every woman who had written a few books and acted the suffragette they would be overloaded with dull features.
>
> . . . If we have had no geniuses in the arts I can't see that it matters very much: there are plenty of international ones to go round. In our isolation, Mr. Gillespie could bring the rest of the world closer by compiling programmes on some of the truly great artists.
>
> It seems a pity we have to call Miss Mander "one of our most important writers" because it only shows our poor source of selection. She is not an important writer, but if she really is one of *our* most important then we should keep it quiet and certainly not broadcast the fact. Why don't we face it? We've never had anyone of real literary worth (I can hear the roar), but after all Miss Mansfield only reads well if one hasn't read Tchekov. . . .[18]

In an editorial, "Who Was Jane Mander?", the journal answered that she "was indeed forthright; more important she was honest about herself as well as other people, and she would never have pretended that she had any claims to genius. . . . But she was one of the first New Zealanders to write novels with a genuine flavour of life in this country. . . . and people who were not young in those days may scarcely imagine the bareness of the literary scene. . . . Moreover Jane Mander's personal story exemplified the struggle of all our writers: the turbulent youth and the frustration, the travels abroad, the attempt to establish an imaginative hold upon a country in which not enough people have lived and died. . . ." The editor continues:

A national literature, modest though it may be, has functions and values which cannot be supplied from outside; and these are not weakened or destroyed because better books have been published elsewhere. Books that are written here are helping us to strengthen our foothold on two islands in the Pacific; they are products of an experience which cannot be complete until it has been lived again in the imagination.

Two attitudes stand in the way: an uncritical enthusiasm which inflates New Zealand writing beyond its true worth, and a sweeping denigration. Between these extremes is, of course, the placid indifference of the multitude, but writers are, or should be, used to it and need not be dismayed. The extremes of opinion are dangerous, not because they silence writers or lift them to a spurious reputation, but because they interfere with critical standards. No attempt has been made to exalt Jane Mander beyond her real achievement. . . . She has been introduced to a new generation of New Zealanders because, apart from her work as a writer, she was an extremely interesting person whose friends remember her with affection and respect. She influenced many people, including younger writers; and her imprint on New Zealand letters, although not deep, is firm and clear. Detraction cannot harm her; but it can harm the rest of us, much more than some of us may realise, if we allow it to pass unchallenged.[19]

"Uncritical enthusiasm" has been a minor problem compared with the more prevalent "sweeping denigration"—an attitude in which critics have often seemed primarily concerned to demonstrate their own acquaintance with "the truly great." When desire for a regional literature came to be felt, some New Zealand critics were guilty of applying yet another pressure: instead of fostering numbers for safety they tended, like ambitious parents of only children, to look for "the great New Zealand novel" from any writer who dared humbly to exist. Most of these obstructions have been dispersed during the 1960's as the thoroughly diverse talents of a number of new novelists have taught the country to rely on a literature rather than on a few named books.

Though technically clumsy compared with some of the moderns, Jane Mander would seem to have gained more than she has lost by becoming part of a concourse. It is one that sees no need to repudiate her; all that is lost is her isolation and her compatriots' naïveté. She is due for rehearing—one might better say that she is overdue for a hearing, as the first one was lost in irrelevancies—and it will be interesting to see what comes of it. Broad popularity is unlikely: she lacks magic, and the rough surface of her style deters the casual or self-indulgent reader. To judge, though, by the respect of younger writers and serious students one might predict the widening of an audience sophisticated enough to cut through the blemishes to the dynamic integrity of her central achievement.

One can see her taking a possibly mistaken direction in her later novels, driven as she was to try various ways of becoming a full-time novelist. Yet the significance of her life may lie most of all in her quite extraordinary grasp of what professionalism implied. Until the last two decades in New Zealand, practitioners in all the arts have had their wry amusement from the dictionary definitions which relate profession to livelihood; in a society offering neither the economy, the framework, the encouragement, nor the competition productive of standards, artists have drawn on their own very solitary resolves first to formulate their aim and then to reach it by spare-time application. It has meant withdrawal—often unrespected and misunderstood—from an otherwise pleasant and friendly society.

Jane Mander took overseas a firm resolve and a practiced capacity for abstention. As Sargeson wrote: "The novelist's craft is surely a strange one: most New Zealanders, I should say, can readily imagine their doing much more exciting things in New York and London than sitting down and re-creating on paper the kauri forests and tidal rivers of North Auckland. Not so Miss Mander, and anyone who visits the North will recognise how close to reality her scenes are. It is this solid realism which is Miss Mander's greatest strength as a writer."[20] New York did indeed give her a thoroughly good time which her popularity and enterprise could have extended indefinitely. In an intense act of will she excluded New York and denied her other talents, keeping the way clear for the facts of New

Zealand to creep in upon her again. She was quite mistimed for her own happiness as a professional New Zealand novelist. "My whole life has been lived round the motiv . . . too late" she wrote in her "Preface to Reminiscences." By present reckoning she was at least thirty years too soon for the appreciation and moral support her writing merited. From yet another viewpoint, her books might be seen as justly timed—as the leading obituary said: "Even a competent novel is a sort of miracle when it comes, unannounced and lonely, to a country with a weak literary tradition."[21] It was a comfortless destiny, perhaps, but one she can be imagined volunteering for if it had to be undertaken by someone.

Notes and References

Chapter One

1. In 1966 Esther Norton Soule, quite unprompted, offered the strongest recollection of Jane Mander's promotion of *The Story of an African Farm* during the New York years, and of her ambition in this regard.

2. The birthplace is now the residence of Mr. and Mrs. Allen Reid, Ramarama, standing a little back from the Great South Road, just north of the clay bank opposite "Raventhorpe." Modernized—the steep roof lowered and the windows squared off—it looks younger than the house next it on the south but is considerably older.

3. André Siegfried, *Democracy in New Zealand* (London, 1914), p. 53. The book appeared originally in French in 1904, soon after the author's visit to New Zealand; reading Siegfried one can't help feeling that Frank Mander was one of the people he had in fact observed.

4. Francis Mander gave his birth year as 1849 in the *Cyclopaedia of New Zealand* (1902) and throughout the editions of *Who's Who in New Zealand*; as these are the standard reference books, the error has spread. The original birth record at the registrar-general's is in perfect order: it was 1848. But in registering the births of his children Francis Mander twice declared himself a year too young; the preoccupations of an abnormal boyhood plainly left him vague, the error settled in. Some time in his old age—the family is unsure when —it was straightened out. The death notices and the obituary in the *Northern Advocate* have it correct, and Jane Mander wrote to Pat Lawlor on December 2, 1941 that he "saw his ninety-third birthday yesterday."

5. George McDonald, editor of the Ararimu centennial booklet, searched the title of every property in the area; I am indebted to him for amplification, and for background to the material published in the booklet.

6. "As a reward for specially good behaviour my mother would open a tin-lined case in which she kept some of the few things that had been overlooked by the Maoris when they wrecked my grand-father's house during the war. Anyone can visualise the contents of that box of Georgian and early Victorian bric-à-brac, needlework, old silver and china and jewellery. There has never been in my life a box more full of enchantment. Even the tissue paper wrappings

were fragrant with the English associations that tug so at the heart of exiles." Jane Mander in the London, *Daily Chronicle*, November 3, 1928.

7. Both Mander and Bradley families have always been proud of the unwritten agreement. Mr. A. E. Allen, M.P. for Franklin, great-nephew of Samuel Bradley, worked as a youth on Bert Mander's farm and has confirmed the prevailing idealism as to the spoken word; he told me also that while all these men expected the able-bodied to work as hard as they did, they had a quite abnormal sense of responsibility toward any unfortunates in their orbit.

8. In the Auckland Institute and Museum Library, filed with the Kaiwaka Centennial papers; also in the Turnbull Library, ref. 18/081.

9. The Kaiwaka school records are lost. Jane Mander's sisters have always believed that she attended this school, as the Gillespie portrait says. Mr. Henry Bowmar, her contemporary, told me in 1964 that he would have remembered her and her brother as school-mates if they had been there regularly. One has only to look at the terrain to see that even such intrepid children would often be defeated by the journey involved.

10. *Cyclopaedia of New Zealand*, Auckland Volume (Christ-church, 1902), p. 421.

11. Jane Mander's headmaster, George Reid, was a fine musician; he was also the village doctor—unqualified, of course, but they all thought the world of him, as they did of Frank Mander who became the village dentist. Mr. Walter Becroft of Port Albert described to me how he rode down one night to have a tooth extracted by Frank Mander, who dabbed the cavity so liberally with laudanum that the boy had to dismount on the way home. (Mention of laudanum in *Allen Adair* and *The River* suggest that it was the local forerunner of aspirin.) Mr. Becroft and Mrs. Smith of Te Hana, both pupils of Jane Mander's at the Port Albert school, remembered her well as a very bright girl and a very proper teacher. A local debating society, in which Jane took part, discussed such subjects as "Machinery," "Is Marriage a Failure?," "Women's Suffrage," and "Smoking." For details of the Albertlanders' social and religious ideals and for their pioneering hardships, see books on Albertland in the bibliography.

12. *Cyclopaedia of New Zealand*, Auckland Volume (Christ-church, 1902), p. 421.

13. He told the House that there were 1,400 miles of railway in the South Island, 750 miles in the North Island south of Auckland, and north of Auckland 100 miles, increasing at the rate of one and a quarter miles per annum. "I have had to go down with the tide sometimes more than nine or ten miles in my boat to meet the

steamer, and when you get there the steamer has frequently not arrived, and you have to wait at the top of the water until she can come up, and then you have to wait until the tide goes out and comes in again before you can get home; and sometimes, when the wind is strong, you are simply stuck there for two or three days at a time." *Journals of the House*, Vol. 123, p. 245. Seddon went north in 1904 and to a deputation in Maungaturoto, and again in Whangarei, said that "where all things were equal it was unreasonable and unnatural to expect the Government to look with the same kindly eye on those returning Opposition members as on those returning Government supporters." There followed by telegraph a public row, in which Seddon tried to wriggle out and Mander accused him of quibbling; the electorate showed its scorn of the government by returning Mander with an increased majority.

14. Biographical note for J. C. Andersen, Alexander Turnbull Library.

15. Now No. 64 Hatea Drive, the house was bought from the Manders by my uncle, A. R. Pickmere, and I spent much of my childhood there. The present owners, Hereward and Nancy Pickmere, have modernized a little, but no repairs have been needed. The tower has been brought down for safety to the front lawn.

16. Mr. Ian Whitwell visiting the *North Auckland Times* office in 1967 was shown the script of an address given by the late C. R. Bagnall, former editor, which mentioned Jane Mander as one of the paper's past editors. The office held four issues of 1908 which had no clues.

17. See Chapter 5, I.

18. Biographical note for J. C. Andersen, Alexander Turnbull Library.

19. The *Mirror*, June 1, 1934.

20. Records in the School of Journalism Library, Columbia University.

21. The application form is on microfilm at Barnard College. Jane Mander's handwriting remained to the end of her life a strong, simple script a school inspector would have approved of in a teacher of young pupils. In a letter to J. H. E. Schroder in 1938 (in the Alexander Turnbull Library) she wrote: "Well now, that is an achievement, recognising my handwriting, for it cannot be that my calligraphy is as distinctive as all that, though I have had it praised twice recently by young men in post offices."

22. John William Cunliffe, D. Litt., had been head of the Department of English at the University of Wisconsin before coming to take charge of written English in the School of Journalism; he had begun life as a reporter in London and Manchester and was now

an expert on Elizabethan and modern British dramatists.

23. *Many a Good Crusade: Memoirs of Virginia Crocheron Gildersleeve* (New York, 1954), p. 98.

24. "New Zealand Novels: The Struggle against Environment," Christchurch *Press*, December 15, 1934.

25. This is part of Miss Meyer's reply to my appeal for recollections; I had found no mention of Jane Mander in Barnard College's very full records of club activities.

26. Letter to A. V. Cross.

27. See the Gillespie Radio Portrait in the Alexander Turnbull Library. It is not known to whom Jane Mander wrote this letter, but it is consistent with what she says in the existing letters quoted above:

28. There is obviously a script being rewritten, though she makes no subsequent mention of having continued work on the novel rejected in London. If Macmillan rejected this revised script at the end of 1913, it would be then that "I scrapped all that copy and in the year the war broke out I began work on the Story of a New Zealand River. I could not work continuously on it, as I was studying at the same time. I kept on at it after the war broke out, as nobody imagined the war would last, but I worked only intermittently on it. . . . Actually I stopped working on the book a little while before America went into the war." (Biographical note for Ethel W. Wilson, September 1, 1938, in the Alexander Turnbull Library.) The biographical note for J. C. Andersen, also in the Turnbull, reads: "I went to London in 1912. I took with me a first novel, not the Story of a New Zealand River, as has been erroneously stated. This book was turned down with admirable promptitude by four publishers. . . .But before long I began writing again, and when the war broke out I had The Story of a New Zealand River planned and partly written. I was determined to finish the book and did so under considerable difficulties. Some time in 1917 I met a friend of John Lane's American manager who persuaded me to let the latter see the manuscript. He liked it and sent it to London with his recommendation. . . . So my Story of a New Zealand River was accepted by the first publisher to whom it was sent." The last sentence clinches the matter; and in this biographical note there is nothing apart from the question of *The River* to account for her saying, in the covering letter to Mr. Andersen, "I will forward you a brief but *accurate* account of my literary career and work for the brochure, for nothing *accurate* has yet appeared about me in any N. Z. paper." The papers had been accurate enough otherwise.

29. Written recollection given me by Mrs. Soule.

30. Radio script in the Auckland Public Library. The Theatre Guild had the world premiere of *Heartbreak House*, and was the

first theater to produce *Back to Methuselah.* "The hard heart of Mr. Bernard Shaw was so moved that he then gave the Theatre Guild the sole rights in America of all his plays, and wrote to the company that if anything could take him to so barbarous a place as New York their work would," Jane Mander says, and one can imagine her delight at being in the Shavian center; but it is Eugene O'Neill she mentions at more length, both here and in the London Letters to the *Sun,* particularly the production of *The Emperor Jones* by the Provincetown Players in 1920, with John Gilpin in the lead.

31. *Ibid.*

32. Mary Gray Peck in her biography of Carrie Chapman Catt (New York, 1944) writes: "During the following months, New York City was the spectacular end of the state and secured the lion's share of the publicity, but the fact of deepest significance was that there was not a cross-roads hamlet from New York to Buffalo, between the St. Lawrence and Lake Ontario and the Pennsylvania Line, that did not have at least one campaign meeting, that was not repeatedly visited by leading women of the country, that was not canvassed house by house, that was not interested by one of the many 'stunts' that were abroad in the land during the summer and fall of 1915."

33. Letter to A. V. Cross.

34. *Utica Daily Press,* July 28 and 29, 1915.

35. Letter to A. V. Cross.

36. Biographical note for E. W. Wilson in the Alexander Turnbull Library.

37. Biographical note for J. C. Andersen in the Alexander Turnbull Library.

38. "Flats for Single Women" in *Time and Tide* (April 25,1924.) Jane Mander pleads for the provision in London of the type of single apartment for working women taken for granted in New York; she rails at London boarding houses and clubs which starve women's homemaking instincts. But "I love London more every day for its birds, beasts, flowers and many other things. . . ."

39. Letter to Pat Lawlor, written May 12, the year not given, but internal evidence points to 1931.

40. Letter to Leonard Moore, Alexander Turnbull Library; dated December 22, no year given, but "I hope that I shall be one of those who add to the prosperity of the firm in 1932." In two other letters of this group of four, written from St. Leonard's-on-sea on March 31 and April 1, she mentions her writing: "I certainly do not want to be bothered with it now that I am swinging along with my own book," and "I refuse to be hurried or to interrupt the work on my own novel for them." Christy and Moore stamped these 1930 on receipt. It appears that work on this seventh novel went on through 1930 and 1931; and late in 1931 she wrote to M. H. Holcroft, "and

who will take it I cannot say. . . . I am hoping to get yet another book what I have started finished before I come." Aboard ship on her way to New Zealand she wrote to him: "My book is held up for revision, and I'm already well into another, which will have to be finished first." Then from Auckland in 1933: "Sometimes I wonder if I shall ever start up again. And yet I have two books almost finished—one I'm devoted to in odd moments." In 1934 she began, presumably, on a third script: "My new novel is going to be set in England, bright as a button and up-to-date. I've learnt my lesson." Then, in response to Mr. Holcroft's alarm at her "bright as a button" attitude, "you need not be alarmed about my new book. It is not up-to-the-minute or 'bright' or anything of the current order. It is set up on the Welsh border where I spent two enchanted summers, in a place that is as much in my blood as anything in New Zealand, and it has nothing to do with London or ephemeral cults and fashions, though it is more or less modern . . . being set in the year 1932. It must be done before I go back to the N. Z. setting, which of course I am going to do later. Don't worry." In 1937 she wrote to him: "But a new book is what I want to do . . . and I really mean to get started on it this winter." Jane Mander is presumed to have destroyed all her unpublished or incomplete scripts, but it is not known when.

41. Derek Patmore, *Private History* (London, 1960.)

42. Letter to me from Derek Patmore.

43. Mr. Monroe Wheeler gave a very helpful interview about Jane Mander and her association with Harrison of Paris, first to Una Platts of Auckland, who kindly passed on her notes, and again in 1966 when I saw him in New York.

44. John Mulgan, *Report on Experience* (London, 1947), p. 10.

45. Ngaio Marsh, "The Background," Christchurch *Press*, December 22, 1934.

46. D'Arcy Cresswell, *Present without Leave* (London, 1939), pp. 250, 215 and 223.

47. This first sheet of a letter with an English address has part of one of Jane Mander's radio scripts typed on the reverse. Using it is, I fear, violation of the principle which impelled her to destroy friends, correspondence; but the writer is unidentifiable, says nothing of him- or herself, and there is nothing else of this kind in the papers.

48. Note written for me by Maud Graham (née Ballantyne).

49. In Auckland Public Library.

50. With Jane Mander's papers in the Auckland Public Library.

51. In Gloria Rawlinson's possession.

52. Letter to Pat Lawlor.

Chapter Two

1. The places named in *The River* all existed, and the story is true to local

contours and distances. But there was never a mill at Pukekaroro nor any such township as the novel portrays—half a dozen houses at most in "the Bay" and the logs floated downstream to be cut elsewhere; the author imported the Puhipuhi mill settlement to make a composite picture. The Rolands' house is placed where the Manders lived at Point Ernie. Access is by road now; just north of Kaiwaka on the Auckland-Whangarei highway a sign calls attention to Mount Pukekaroro on the eastern side, reserve for regenerating kauri. The first western side road north of Kaiwaka—ironically signposted "School Bus Route"—gives at once a view of Point Ernie, and better views a mile or two in. The piles of the original timber tramline are still upright in the mud; just above these, in a field running up from the beach, a power pylon stands where "the Boss's" house was. About three-tenths of a mile down this side road indentations in the fields show the tramline's route down from the heights. Mrs. Brayton's house is visible behind pine trees on the heights above the river to the south, the property now of Mr. S. V. Mills whose farm runs back to the main highway.

Mrs. Brayton is drawn from Mrs. Clayton, a wealthy Englishwoman who lived there in Jane Mander's childhood, died in 1895 and is buried in St. Helen's churchyard at Hakaru. Mr. Henry Bowmar who worked for her as a boy remembered clearly her wonderful garden, her houseful of treasures and many birds—there was always a parrot on her shoulder. "Was she likeable?" I asked him. "She was likeable to the people she liked; people knew when she didn't like them. But she was a good woman." On the reissue of *The River* the reviewer for the Dunedin *Evening Star* (August 13, 1938) used his space to talk of the "rabid interest" the Kaiwaka district took in the book when first published: "The older inhabitants announced with laughter or anger according to their individual temperaments that not only could they recognise the setting and the life which they all admitted were accurate beyond question, they also identified each of the characters with past and present residents of the district." Jane Mander wrote to Pat Lawlor that this "amused me very much, as no characters whatever were taken from the district except the fine old lady who could not possibly have objected. Indeed she was dead long before I wrote the book, and her son, who lives near us in Remuera, has always been delighted with the picture I made of her. Also I was only nine when we left that place, and we never had any mill or village there, and a whole new generation had grown up when the book was written. So it is most amusing how people will try all wrongly to fit persons they know into a book."

2. To J. H. E. Schroder, June, 1938, in the Alexander Turnbull Library.

3. Gillespie Radio Portrait, Alexander Turnbull Library, presumably quoted from a letter.

4. In her regular contribution to the *Athenaeum*, on July 9, 1920, Katherine Mansfield mated *The River* and another first novel—*A Child of the Alps*, by Margaret Symonds—as a starting point for some general observa-

tions on the novelist's problems. She concluded with a lengthy and percep-
tive consideration of *The River*—the only serious review that any New
Zealander gave this book at the time. The whole article was republished in
Novels and Novelists (London, 1930; pp. 217-19) in the uniform edition of
Katherine Mansfield's works, and is substantially reproduced here as that
volume is out of print. The review begins:

We question whether anyone who has not himself written the eighty thousand-odd
words realises to the full the grim importance of the fact that a novel is not written
in a day. In the case of the short story it is possible to give orders that, unless the house
is on fire—and even then, not until the front staircase is well alight—one must not
be disturbed; but a novel is an affair of weeks, of months; time after time the author
is forced to leave what he has written today exposed to what may happen before
tomorrow. How can one measure the influence of the interruptions and distrac-
tions that come between? How can one be certain of the length of time that one's
precious idea will wait for one? And then, suppose the emotional atmosphere is re-
captured and the new link forged, there is always the chance that memory may play
one false as to what is already written. The painter places his canvas on the easel;
he steps away, he takes a long absorbed look, and it is all there before him from the
first stroke to the last. But the author cannot go back to Chapter I and read again;
he has no means of constantly renewing his knowledge of what he has actually
written as opposed to what he has come to take for granted is there. And who shall
say it is easy, in the final moment of relief and triumph, when the labourer's task
is o'er and he knows all, to begin to be critical on such a point?

Katherine Mansfield then remarks that neither of these two first novelists
seems sensible that "there might be danger in the leisurely style." Miss
Symonds indeed writes with "a strange confidence"; her smooth, frail
novel lies snugly within the shelter of a strong tradition. "It is," says Katherine Mansfield, "as though we listened to this gentle, well-bred book,
rather than read it," and she turns to Jane Mander's novel, almost its
antithesis.

The case of Miss Jane Mander is very different. Her "Story of a New Zealand
River," which takes four hundred and thirty-two pages of small type to tell, has none
of Miss Symonds' sophistication, or European atmosphere. The scene is laid in the
back blocks of New Zealand, and, as is almost invariably the case with novels that
have a colonial setting, in spite of the fact that there is frequent allusion to the magnificent scenery, it profiteth us nothing. "Stiff laurel-like puriris stood beside the
drooping lace fringe of the lacy rimu; hard blackish kahikateas brooded over the oak-
like ti-toki with its lovely scarlet berry." What picture can that possibly convey to
an English reader? What emotion can it produce? But that brings us to the fact that
Miss Jane Mander is immensely hampered in her writing by her adherence to the old
unnecessary technical devices—they are no more—with which she imagines it necessary to support her story. If one has the patience to persevere with her novel, there
is, under all the false wrappings, the root of something very fresh and sturdy. She
lacks confidence and the courage of her opinions; like the wavering, fearful heroine,

she leans too hard on England. There are moments when we catch a bewilderingly vivid glimpse of what she really felt and knew about the small settlement of people in the lumber-camp, but we suspect that these are moments when she is off her guard. Then her real talent flashes out; her characters move quickly, almost violently; we are suddenly conscious what an agony, what an anguish it was to Bruce when he felt one of his drunken fits coming on; or The Boss reveals his extraordinary simplicity when he tells his wife he thought she'd been unfaithful to him for years.

But these serve nothing but to increase our impatience with Miss Mander. Why is her book not half as long, twice as honest? What right has she to bore her readers if she is capable of interesting them? It would be easy to toss "The Story of a New Zealand River" aside and to treat it as another unsuccessful novel, but we have been seeking for pearls in such a prodigious number of new books that we are forced to the conclusion that it is useless to dismiss any that contain something that might one day turn into a pearl. What is extremely impressive to the novel reviewer is the modesty of the writers—their diffidence in declaring themselves what they are—their almost painful belief that they must model themselves on somebody. We turn over page after page wondering numbly why this unknown he or she should go through the labour of writing all this down. They cannot all of them imagine that this book is going to bring them fame and fortune. And then—no, not always, but a great deal more often than the cultivated public would believe—there is a sentence, there is a paragraph, a whole page or two, which starts in the mind of the reviewer the thrilling thought that this book was written because the author wanted to write. How is this timidity to be explained, then? One would imagine that round the corner there was a little band of jeering, sneering, superior persons ready to leap up and laugh if the cut of the new-comer's jacket is not of the strangeness they consider admissible. In the name of the new novel, the new sketch, the new story, if they are really there, let us defy them.

5. Jane Mander used to tell overseas interviewers she had been a barefoot child and they made much of it; but it was usual in the north: there were no venomous flora or fauna, no ice, mud was the enemy, shoes were silly. Mr. Edgar Hames told me that he had no shoes in the Kaipara, even for church, until an important aunt from England was imminent; shoes were ordered but arrived on the same coach as the aunt; the boys were shuffled out of sight to put them on, appeared with them on the wrong feet, were shuffled off again, but young Edgar reappeared to ask the company "Does it matter which feet the socks go on?" Many urban northerners too go barefoot around their places for comfort and let the children go barefoot to school; it has been found that the simplest way of sizing up new immigrants is to see how they take this: if they think it awful they will apply a rigid, parochially determined set of values to more important matters. But Jane Mander seems to have noticed this long ago.

6. Timber men always spoke of "a bush," meaning an area of bush, and Jane Mander followed suit naturally: e.g., "I could not begin to put into books all the 'unrepresentative' people we came across in the bushes, about the gumfields. . . ." But this has not come into ordinary usage; we say "the bush" or "a bit of bush," and for the plural "bits of bush" or "bush areas."

7. Joan Stevens, *The New Zealand Novel: 1860-1865* (Wellington, 1966), p. 37.

8. Reviewers have almost unanimously taken Alice as the central figure, but in the *New Zealand Herald*'s initial review, pasted on the first page of Jane Mander's album, the word "central" is underlined in ink and is followed by what looks like an exclamation or question mark, though there is no way of knowing whether this was done by her or the person who sent it from New Zealand.

9. M. H. Holcroft, "The Facts of Fiction," editorial in the *New Zealand Listener*, January 13, 1961.

10. "Sheltered Daughters," *New Republic*, June 24, 1916.

11. Frank Sargeson, "North Auckland Story," *Auckland Star*, June 25, 1938.

12. See note 4, above.

13. Unsigned review in *Tomorrow*, August 3, 1938.

Chapter Three

1. See article on Puhipuhi in *Resources of New Zealand*, an illustrated promotional survey of the north published by Alderton and Wyatt, Whangarei (1907).

2. David E. Hutchins, *New Zealand Forestry Part I: Kauri Forests and Forests of the North and Forest Management* (Government Printer, Wellington, 1919), p. 55.

3. *New Zealand*: Painted by F. and W. Wright, Described by Honorable William Pember Reeves (London, 1918), p. 102.

4. "My Life in Two Worlds," article in the London *Daily Chronicle*, November 3, 1928.

5. M. H. Holcroft, *Creative Problems in New Zealand* (Christchurch, 1948), p. 21.

6. Frank Sargeson in "North Auckland Story" in the *Auckland Star*, June 25, 1938.

7. In the *New Republic*, June 24, 1916. One extract is in Chapter 2; the following may be more applicable to Valerie:

The sheltered daughter is to be found in all kinds of homes where economic pressure has not found its way. She is one of the crimes for which poverty is not responsible. She may be preserved for various ends, of which the three most clearly defined are the marriage market, safety in "the hands of the Lord," and the comfort and use of her parents.

The first of these obviously originated with the woman-as-property idea. The various grades of "Society" in city and village still regard marriage to money and position as the be-all and end-all of life for their women, and to that end daughters must be bred in the manner desired by the men of their own particular set. This manner must include the accomplishments valued by each particular circle, adherence to the set's habits and conventions, and, above all, inconspicuousness. . . .

If my parents have, for twenty years, saved, schemed, plotted, gone without opera tickets and an automobile, pursued influential friends, lain awake at night thinking out how to make one dollar do the work of two, in order to send me through finishing schools, European trips, and sun baths on Palm Beach, with a view to my marriage to a title or a steel magnate, if after all this, I refuse to be a débutante, and caught by a vision of usefulness, I take to suffrage and soap boxes, to *The Masses* and Emma Goldman, it really is a sad business for my parents. What is to be done about it?

The whole trouble, it seems to me, lies in our tenacious belief in the supreme excellence of ourselves, our circle, our church, our way. Of course if I believe that my beliefs, my tastes, my habits, my conventions, are the only right or desirable ones in the world, then naturally I must try to impose them on my child. I must employ the methods of the Inquisition to save her mind and soul. . . .

But if I believe, as I ought to, that I hold my beliefs, my conventions, my habits and my tastes, simply because they happen to appeal to my own particular mental and physical make-up, then I have no right to assume that my child must hold them too. The only intelligent thing for me to do is to look for difference, and to be interested in it. And if I want her friendship, as I always say I do, I must be the sort of person with whom she can compare notes upon the way.

In short, the only way that I can keep my child is to give up every claim upon her; to cease, in fact, to take advantage of the accident by which nature made me her parent.

8. Even the scenery was despised. Ngaio Marsh, a much-traveled South Islander, has a poke at the southern attitude in *Colour Scheme* (London, 1943), p. 47. An English actor is being driven to a northern holiday retreat and says:

". . .For pity's sake, my dear Dikon, drive a little farther away from the edge of the abyss. Can this mountain goat-track possibly be a main road?"

"It's the only road from Harpoon to Wai-ata-tapu, sir. You wanted somewhere quiet, you know. And these are not mountains. There are no mountains in Northland. The big stuff is in the south."

"I'm afraid you're a scenic snob. To me this is a mountain. When I fall over the edge of this precipice, I shall not be found with a sneer on my lips because the drop was merely five hundred feet instead of a thousand."

9. W. J. Gardner's article on "The Reform Party" in *Ends and Means in New Zealand Politics* (University of Auckland Bulletin No. 60, 1961), p. 27.

10. Letter to John A. Lee, Auckland Public Library.

11. *Ibid.*

12. Frank Sargeson, "North Auckland Story," *Auckland Star*, June 25, 1938.

13. The setting is literally true to the tiny port of Pahi, but not beyond, because a journey back up the narrow tongue of land behind Pahi would encounter the already considerable settlement of Paparoa and could not therefore place the Adairs in the stipulated isolation. Mr. Edgar Hames of

Paparoa surmises that Jane Mander had in mind a field on the other side of the Pahi River, behind Whakapirau, in the Marohemo region—something in the social and physical flavor of the novel suggests this to him. This would bring Allen Adair's gumfield closer to the area of *The River*, which Jane Mander probably revisited by boat in her Dargaville days. The likelihood is that she deliberately transposed physical features and mileages in such a way as to defy literal identification with any one place.

Chapter Four

1. Jane Mander writing from London in the Auckland *Sun*, November 23, 1928.

2. Biographical note for Ethel W. Wilson in the Alexander Turnbull Library.

3. William Pember Reeves in *The Long White Cloud* (London, 1924), pp. 313-14.

4. See editorial in the *Auckland Star*, September 14, 1968: "There is already a good deal of scattered evidence that they are not happy at all. The most startling indication is the rising rate of mental breakdown among suburban housewives. Four times as many women as men suffer from depression acute enough to bring them into psychiatric hands. Dr. D. M. F. McDonald, superintendent of Kingseat, is an outspoken critic of the social forces that lie behind this development. He has called women the 'Negroes' of New Zealand society. . . ."

Chapter Five

1. Jane Mander returned to New Zealand in 1932 with an English publisher's contract for her reminiscences and in 1938 was still hoping to get on with this book. Circumstances defeated her, and she left behind none of the notes she is thought to have assembled for it. The following, on one typed page, was on its own in her box of clippings (the ellipses and spellings are hers):

Preface to Reminiscences. . .

Book sent to John Lane's manager by glamorous young man, one of Roosefeldt's young men whose name I regret to say I have forgotten. It is sad to think how many names one does forget. And of those I remember best I can say least, for their stories fascinating are their own. I don't claim to have been told more secrets than any other woman, but I do claim to have kept more secrets than most women, and those who have confided them to me may be sure they will still be kept.

I was intended to play the role of being visible in the background, as Rom Landau puts it. . .I love looking on at life much more than strutting about in it. I should love parties if only I could sit in a corner, knowing everyone present, or at least who they are, and watch the comedy and the farce. . .I ought to have been born a rich woman, or at any rate a well to do one. I should have made, if trained, quite a decent patron of the arts, and an encourager of the young, especially the talented and beautiful young. I have always been far more interested in other people's work than in my own. That is why I have been a very minor novelist and owner of most of the world's best novels by other people. In that I have been entirely frustrated. I might have made a good Beethoven player. I have large powerful rugged hands. But I had nothing but a cracked harmonium to play on till I was able to afford a piano, and then it was too late. My whole life has been lived round the motiv. . .too late. I went to school too late to earn a scholarship. I developed too late to be blessed or destroyed by marriage. I left home and N. Z. too late to establish myself in England before the war broke out. I developed a critical sense too late, studied art too late, loved everybody too late, always saw jokes too late and all because I insisted on living in a private world of my own from which I was eternally being jerked to miss the right second. . . .

2. Christchurch *Press* on November 10, 17, and 24; December 1, 8, and 15, 1934.

3. *Triad*, October 19, 1923.

4. The only pre-1916 clipping in Jane Mander's file is an undated article on the Sydney Children's Court, which Mr. H. Roth of the Auckland University Library identified at once as from the *Maoriland Worker*; a search of files revealed an article on "Labour in Australia," of June 2, 1911, and "A Woman's View," quoted below. It is likely that she contributed also to two other Wellington Labour publications—*The Commonweal*, and the *Weekly Herald*. Library holdings of these are scattered and sketchy, some on almost undecipherable microfilm, but a long-range hunt could turn up more of "Manda Lloyd."

5. *Maoriland Worker*, November 24, 1911.

6. *Ibid.*, July 21, 1911.

7. Ivy Elizabeth Farr in *Centennial of Albertland* (Wellsford, 1962), p. 103.

8. Frank Mander inscribed poems in friends' books or gave them ready printed; this is from a late booklet in the Alexander Turnbull Library:

> The world is all unhinged today,
> And creaks from zone to zone,
> But surely man is all to blame,
> Since God he did disown.

· · · · · · · ·

> Gal. 6:7. It is a law infallible,
> That surely all must know,
> We each must reap in after life,
> What in early life we sow.

A DIARY OF EVOLUTION
In a Small Country Town

9. Age.

5-12 Accept Bible as written, God, Christ, and The Angels in toto, Fixed Heaven and Hell, the Good and the Bad.

12-14 Believe Bible "inspired," but not all "literal." Shed Fixed Hell. See Satan as force of Evil. Doubt Divinity of Christ.

14-16 Read Bible as history and legend. Shed Divinity of Christ, and The Angels. Keep God as Love, Justice, and Father of Mankind. Have fixed ideas of Right and Wrong, but become interested in the Bad.

16-18 Browning stage. Frame "God's in His Heaven, All's Right With the World." Parade aggressive Optimism. Accept "World as it is." Preach Duty of Cheerfulness, etc. Orthodox as to Poverty and the Working Classes.

18-19 Honest Doubt. Learn Omar Khayyam by heart. Shed Heaven. Question Personal God. Put away "God's in His Heaven." More liberal as to sin.

19-22 General mental tangle. Study Theosophy and Reincarnation, Spiritualism and Christian Science. Shed Personal God. Call Him Force, the First Cause, the Guiding Principle, Universal Law, etc. Believe in Mind Over Matter, and Love as Constructive Force. Shed fixed ideas of Right and Wrong. See Sin as Defective Education. Morality the new religion. Frame Henley's "Invictus." Exalt the Self. Believe in Human Nature. Get first glimmer of Evolution. Hear vaguely of Socialism. Realize the Brotherhood of Man with due regard for Classes and Types.

In New York

22-23 Discover Bernard Shaw. Shed everything else.

23-25 Plunge into psychology, biology, history. Doubt everything but Scientific Facts. Shed God in any form. Learn the Relativity of Truth. Meet Socialists. Investigate Sex War and Wage War. Have Temperament. Exalt the Intellect. Despise the Average Person. Put "Invictus" away in a drawer.

25-26 Begin again. The new religion—socialism—; the new god—humanity; the new Christ—the man, the carpenter; the new devils—poverty, capitalism; the new heaven and hell—the earth; the new Bible—Marx, Wells, the Fabian Society, The Economists; the new sins—ignorance, indifference; the new temples—the street corner, the lecture hall; the new idealism—liberté, egalité, fraternité; the new words —Individualism, Communism, Humanitarianism.

26-28 Preach Radicalism, Anarchism, Agitation, and No Compromise. Despise Laws, Ceremonies, Traditions, and Precedents. Believe in Free Love. Exalt Sincerity. Proclaim The Facts of Life. Lose temperament in a flurry of general destruction. Tolerate all Comrades in the March of Progress. Believe in The People and the Natural Rights of Man.

28-30 Doubt adequacy of Anarchism. Begin to suspect The People. Consider Organization, Cooperation and Education. Study Unions and Statistics. See need for Some Compromise. Shed Anarchism and Agitation.

30-32 Join a union. Believe in the Wage War. Preach Unity and Sacrifice for the Good of All. Lead Strikes.

32-33 Doubt possibility of Unity. Suspect motives of leaders. Question effectiveness of Sacrifice. Hazy as to definition of The Good of All. Lose illusions about The People. See hope in Political Action. Shed Unions and The Working Man.

33-34 Go into politics. Learn the value of Compromise. Suspect the wisdom of Sin-

cerity. Drop Free Love. Uphold Laws and Ceremonies. Hide The Facts of Life.
Try Merit and Reason upon the Politician. Suspect the power of Merit and Reason.
Try Money and Influence upon the politician. Perceive their immediate and
decisive effect. Suspect possibility of Democracy as defined by Lincoln. Suspect
the politician. Suspect myself. Begin to feel tired.
34-35 Shed politics and the politicians. Turn to Social Service. Join four Clubs
and three Movements. Boost the Feminists and Suffragists. Talk, and listen to talk.
Begin to suspect Movements. Suspect all Human Nature. Get more tired.
35-36 A great weariness. Sick of Action. Sick of Words. Sick of Humanity. No illusions left. Shed everything. Do nothing. Turn to Art.
36-37 Believe in Art. Recover Temperament, but don't mention it. Fall in love with
an artist. Believe in love. Believe in the artist. Get married.
37 Have a child who will begin it all over again.

Jane Mander.
(From The *New Republic*, March 25, 1916.)

10. Henry Brett and Henry Hook, *The Albertlanders* (Auckland, 1927),
p. 86.

11. Painted by John Martin, K.L., engraved by Charles Mottram, this
edition published by Thomas McLean, Haymarket, London, in 1857 (which
would make it a very new picture when the Kerrs brought it to New Zealand). Jane Mander's young uncle, Walter, stepped out of whatever shadow
this picture threw into a gentle, cosmic philosophy, printing verses in which
the aspirations and achievements of all ages join modern science as an
evolutionary force which will enable man to perfect himself.

12. Dennis McEldowney in "Ultima Thule to Little Bethel," *Landfall*,
March, 1966.

13. "My Life in Two Worlds," *Daily Chronicle*, November 3, 1928.

14. *Ibid.*

15. See Jane Mander's article on Henry Handel Richardson in the *Bookman*, May, 1929; also "Women Writers I Have Known" in the *Mirror*,
January, 1933.

16. "Creative Writing in Australia and New Zealand" in the *Literary
Digest International Book Review*, May, 1923.

17. *Ibid.*

18. "New Zealand Novelists," Christchurch *Press*, November 17, 1934.

19. See Chapter 2, note 4.

20. Christchurch *Press*, November 24, 1934.

21. A. R. D. Fairburn in *Art in New Zealand*, June, 1934.

22. Robin Hyde in "New Zealand Authoresses" in the *Mirror*, February,
1938.

23. Jane Mander's book page in the *Mirror*, April, 1936.

24. Letter to Pat Lawlor.

25. Phillip Wilson in *The Maorilander* (Christchurch, 1960), p. 96.

26. Henry James's essay, "The Future of the Novel," republished in *Selected Literary Criticism* (London, 1963), p. 225.

27. Christchurch *Press*, December 15, 1934.

28. London letter in the Christchurch *Sun*, February 18, 1927.

29. In the New York *Sun*, March 22, 1922, Jane Mander discussed on the women's page whether the heroines of New Zealand novels would do for American books: "I have asked myself, since reading 'Main Street', if our small towns develop Carol Kennicotts. . . .We have numerous small towns, each with its own peculiar brand of smugness, but they are picturesque and often beautiful small towns, and they can boast a fair variety of human per thousand, though not the variety that results from the immigration America allows. . . . The population of New Zealand is largely middle class English, educated, sport loving. But the beauty of the country, the climate, the possibilities for sport and the freer life have attracted all types of cultivated English people, so much so that I have never been in a small town that had not a few distinctive spirits. A young person thirsting like Carol Kennicott for the higher life and leadership therein would find in any of our towns congenial souls and some cultured people a long way ahead of her. . . ." (The ellipses are Jane Mander's.)

30. Radio script, Auckland Public Library.

31. See note 2 above.

32. Reviewing Margaret Jepson's novel, *Via Panama*, in the *Mirror*, October 1, 1934, Jane Mander wrote:

Touchy New Zealanders will resent a certain attitude to this country that crops out now and again. I must quote the following:
'They've got the village mind in New Zealand . . .'
'But they can't be stupider than most people are at home.'
'They aren't. They're more intelligent on an average. But they're not in the least interested in things. Intellectually and emotionally the average New Zealander is about as fertile as his own boots.'
'You don't make it sound very exciting.'
'Exciting! It couldn't be duller. And I don't suppose you can bake cakes.'
'No, I can't. That is, I never have. Can't one buy them in New Zealand?'
'Yes.'
'But what do cakes matter?'
'There you are, you see! You aren't fit to go to New Zealand.'
'Do they eat a lot of cake?'
'They live on it; and they don't ask questions about it either.'
Considering that there has been a persistent and widespread conspiracy since I returned to my native town to kill me with cake, mental as well as material, I can vouch for the artistic verity of the above piece of dialogue.

33. John Mulgan, *Report on Experience* (London, 1947), p. 10.

34. Ngaio Marsh, "The Background." Christchurch *Press*, December 22, 1934.

35. R. A. Copland in "The Goodly Roof," *Landfall*, September, 1968.

36. Joan Stevens, *The New Zealand Novel: 1860-1965* (Wellington, 1966), p. 38.

37. Ngaio Marsh, *op. cit.*

38. Robert Chapman in "Fiction and the Social Pattern," *Landfall*, March, 1953.

39. "My Life in Two Worlds," London *Daily Chronicle*, November 3, 1928.

40. Alan Mulgan in *Great Days in New Zealand Writing* (Wellington, 1962), p. 88.

41. William Satchell, *The Toll of the Bush* (London, 1905), p. 173.

42. See Keith Sinclair, *A History of New Zealand* (London, 1959), pp. 223-5.

43. "New Zealand Novelists," Christchurch *Press*, November 18, 1934.

Chapter Six

1. Janet Frame, "This Desirable Property": radio talk reprinted in the *New Zealand Listener*, July 3, 1964.

2. There is perhaps no simple explanation of New Zealand's lapse of spirit in the first decades of this century, but readers are referred to Paul W. Day's discussion of the 1920's and his interesting analogy with "bush sickness" in *John Mulgan* (TWAS 58,) pp. 99-100.

3. *New Zealand Herald*, August 14, 1920.

4. *Dominion*, August 28, 1920.

5. The later novels were also stamped "Reserve" and put out of reach; but as a result of withholding *The Passionate Puritan* for some years, Whangarei Public Library is now apparently the only library in the country with a copy in circulation—it is much in demand by school children working on local history.

6. *New Zealand Listener* (editorial), January 13, 1961.

7. For the peculiar difficulties of marketing books in New Zealand see Alan Mulgan in *Literature and Authorship in New Zealand* (P.E.N. Books, 1943), pp. 47-50.

8. *New York Times Book Review*, June 12, 1921.

9. *Dominion*, September 9, 1922.

10. *Evening Post*, September 1, 1923.

11. *Dominion*, October 6, 1923.

12. *New Zealand Herald*, October 25, 1923.

13. *Auckland Star*, September 29, 1923.

14. *Auckland Star*, February 9, 1924.

15. *London Mercury*, July, 1925.

16. Christchurch *Sun*, December 4, 1924.

17. Quoted in "Robin Hyde" by Gloria Rawlinson, in *The Wooden*

Horse, Vol. I., No. 4 (Lawrence, 1950).

18. *New Zealand Listener*, June 17, 1955.

19. *Ibid.*, editorial by M. H. Holcroft.

20. Frank Sargeson, "North Auckland Story," *Auckland Star*, June 25, 1938.

21. M. H. Holcroft, editorially in the *New Zealand Listener*, January 13. 1950.

Selected Bibliography

PRIMARY SOURCES

1. Novels

The Story of a New Zealand River. New York: John Lane Company, 1920; London: John Lane, the Bodley Head, 1920; London: Robert Hale & Company with Whitcombe & Tombs Ltd., New Zealand, 1938 and 1960.

The Passionate Puritan. New York: John Lane Company, 1921; London: John Lane, The Bodley Head, 1922.

The Strange Attraction. New York: Dodd, Mead & Company, 1922; London: John Lane, The Bodley Head, 1923.

Allen Adair. London: Hutchinson & Company, 1925; Auckland: Auckland University Press; London and New York: Oxford University Press, 1971.

The Besieging City. London: Hutchinson & Company, 1926.

Pins and Pinnacles. London: Hutchinson & Company, 1928.

2. Memoirs, articles, reviews, sketches

Three unpublished autobiographical notes are: "Preface to Reminiscences" (400 words) in the Auckland Public Library; Notes (500 words) written in 1938 for Ethel W. Wilson and Notes (800 words) written for Johannes C. Andersen in 1935, both of these in the Alexander Turnbull Library. No comprehensive autobiographical memoir seems to have been published, but two light personal articles with useful angles are with the papers in the Auckland Public Library: "My Life in Two Worlds," *Daily Chronicle*, November 3, 1928; and "No Flappers in New Zealand," *New York Sun*, March 22, 1922, besides numerous fragments and interviews.

The Auckland Public Library papers include the short serial novel, *The Ghost's Warning, Daily Express*, July 11, 12, 14, and 15, 1924, and a number of short, light-weight sketches for English dailies and magazines; two articles from the *New Republic*, "A Diary of Evolution: in a Small Country Town," March 25, 1916, and "Sheltered Daughters," June 24, 1916; "Creative Writing in Australia and New Zealand," *Literary Digest International Book Review*, 1923; "Flats for Single Women," *Time and Tide*, April 25, 1924; the London letters contributed intermittently to the Auckland *Sun* and Christchurch *Sun*; her book page for the *Mirror*, 1934-37, and for *Monocle*, 1938-39; the Christchurch *Press* series, "New Zealand Novelists" on November 10,

159

17, and 24, "New Zealand Novels," December 1 and 8, and "Short Stories: Scope for Dominion Writers," December 15, 1934. This collection includes Jane Mander's scrapbook of reviews of her novels, with some posthumous additions.

3. Letters

Those to her sister, Mrs. A. V. Cross, are now in Mrs. J. B. Walker's possession, and Mr. Pat Lawlor of Wellington holds those written to him; the letters to Mr. John A. Lee are in the Auckland Public Library. Letters to Mr. Leonard Moore, Mr. J. H. E. Schroder, Mr. J. C. Andersen, and Mrs. Ethel W. Wilson are in the Alexander Turnbull Library.

SECONDARY SOURCES

BARLOW, P. W. *Kaipara: or Experience of a Settler in North New Zealand.* London: Sampson & Low, 1888. Entertaining account by an Englishman of the area in the period of *The River.*

BORROWS, J. L. *Albertland; the Last Organised British Settlement in New Zealand.* Wellington: A. H. & A. W. Reed, 1969. New, comprehensive account of the area with good maps.

BRETT, SIR HENRY and HOOK, HENRY. *The Albertlanders: Brave Pioneers of the '60's.* (Auckland: Brett Publishing Co., 1927.) History of the Special Settlement in the Kaipara. Out of print but available in most libraries in New Zealand.

BUTLER, DICK. *This Valley in the Hills.* Whangarei: Northern Publishing Co., 1963. Maungaturoto Centennial history, covering the *Allen Adair* country through to *The River,* with excellent detail of everyday life and photographs.

CHAPMAN, ROBERT. "Fiction and the Social Pattern: Some Implications of Recent New Zealand Writing." *Landfall,* March, 1953. Contains an analysis of the religious and political background of the main body of British immigration, very relevant to Jane Mander's writing.

CHAPMAN, ROBERT et al. *Ends and Means in New Zealand Politics.* University of Auckland, 1961. Six historical lectures lucidly relating political parties to the electorate's motives and ideas: Chapman on "The Decline of the Liberals," and Gardner on "The Reform Party" help place Jane Mander's outlook.

CURNOW, ALLEN. Introduction to *Penguin Book of New Zealand Verse.* London: 1960. Profound study of New Zealand writing, though based on poetry has philosophical implications for prose. Contains also a separate note on pronunciation of Maori words.

FARR, IVY ELIZABETH. *Centennial of Albertland.* Wellsford: Campbell Press, 1962. Good regional history of Port Albert and environs.

GILLESPIE, O. A. Biographical entry on Jane Mander in *An Encyclopaedia of*

New Zealand. Excellent estimate of the author.

———— "Jane Mander: A Radio Portrait." Alexander Turnbull Library, Wellington holds copy of this script broadcast in 1955: dramatized documentary built from letters and from Mr. Gillespie's acquaintance with Jane Mander. Subsequent material shows some details incorrect, but it is an essentially truthful, very illuminating picture.

HUTCHINS, D. E. *New Zealand Forestry Part I: Kauri Forests and Forests of the North and Forest Management*. Wellington: Government Printer, 1919. Booklet primarily for professional use but comprehensible to laymen, written with much descriptive force by leading expert.

KEENE, FLORENCE. *Between Two Mountains: A History of Whangarei*. Auckland: Whitcombe & Tombs, 1966. The first comprehensive study of the district.

LINNELL, R. T. V. *Centennial of Kaiwaka, 1859-1959*. Wellsford: Campbell Press, 1959. Solid, excellently researched booklet of the area of *The River*; useful detail of social customs, Frank Mander timber operations, and so on. Illustrated. Out of print, but in New Zealand libraries.

McCORMICK, E. H. *New Zealand Literature: A Survey*. London: Oxford University Press, 1959. Revision and extension of the relevant part of *Letters and Art in New Zealand*. Wellington: Department of Internal Affairs, 1940. The standard work on the subject.

McDONALD, GEORGE. *They Chose This Valley*. Ararimu: Centennial Committee, 1967. Good regional history of area where Jane Mander was born.

PECK, MARY GRAY. *Carrie Chapman Catt: A Biography*. New York: H. W. Wilson Company, 1944. A history of the suffrage movement in U.S.A. with good coverage of the 1915 campaign in which Jane Mander took part.

REED, A. H. *The Story of the Kauri*. Wellington: A. H. & A. W. Reed, 1953.

———— *The New Story of the Kauri*. Wellington: A. H. & A. W. Reed, 1964. With illustrations by Tudor Collins and others. Full and expert coverage of bush-felling techniques with magnificent photos. Both Mr. Reed and Mr. Collins are veterans of the craft.

———— *The Gumdigger: The Story of Kauri Gum*. Wellington: A. H. & A. W. Reed, 1948. This author spent much of his youth in the gum fields; the book is excellent on both human and technical aspects.

REID, J. C. *Creative Writing in New Zealand: A Brief Critical History*. Auckland: Whitcombe & Tombs, 1946. Stimulating, informative, and in relation to Jane Mander rather provocative.

SIEGFRIED, ANDRE. *Democracy in New Zealand*. London: Bell & Sons, 1914. Translated from the French edition of 1904. Succinct analysis, by visiting Frenchman, of New Zealand character and beliefs circa 1904; almost essential for understanding Jane Mander's background.

SINCLAIR, KEITH. *A History of New Zealand*. London: Penguin, 1959. General history most cognisant of literature and social attitudes.

SMITH, E. M. *A History of New Zealand Fiction; from 1862 to the present time with some account of its relation to national life and character.* Wellington: A. H. & A. W. Reed, 1939. Particularly good on early women novelists and the social milieu; full bibliography of fiction from 1862 to 1939.

STALLWORTHY, JOHN. *Early Northern Wairoa.* Dargaville: Wairoa Bell, 1916. History of the area by proprietor of the *Wairoa Bell* and member of Parliament for Kaipara—both in Jane Mander's time.

STEVENS, JOAN. *The New Zealand Novel: 1860-1965.* Wellington: A. H. & A. W. Reed, 1966. Interesting and comprehensive treatment with excellent section on Jane Mander.

WALL, ARNOLD. *New Zealand English.* Christchurch: Whitcombe & Tombs, 1938. Gives the origin and development of what idiosyncrasies New Zealand speech had up to that date.

Index